5 Steps to Solo Travel

A woman's guide to travel in her prime

Dr. Mary Travelbest

DEDICATION

Dedicated to the women travelers who have blazed the path before us and to those who will continue to do so in the days ahead.

Reviews:

I was intrigued by Dr. Travelbest's honesty and sometimes hilarious lessons learned (you can't make this stuff up). Her clever approach to organizing topics based on STEPS of experience was very helpful to me reading through her book. – S. Holloway

This is a mind opening, very interesting read. I had a very good time working on this project—from start to finish. As I edited, I paused at one point and looked up "Mary Beth McCabe" on the internet, because I wanted to know more about the author. I saw a woman with a radiant smile, and indeed, an eye with adventure sparkling in it. I've learned a lot. Prior to this book, I knew little to nothing about the US. Finally, editing this book made me make one decision. When I've made enough money, I will go on a trip to another African country for a start—maybe Ghana, as a level two traveler. Thank you for granting me this life changing opportunity and believing in me. – Cynthia Nnadi (Nigeria)

You've done a masterful job with this travel book – it is so comprehensive, informative and also fun and easy to read! I've read through it all. What I liked in particular: The five steps of traveling, sustainable travel info (I belong to the Sierra Club, so this is important), and lessons learned. – Pat Rarus, MS

This book is awesome. Brings real-life perspective rather than just words. My favorite section is LESSONS LEARNED! – Cindy Borges

For those of you who love the adventure of traveling alone and those of you who would love to do it but have not yet gotten up the guts to buy that ticket, I have good news for you. Finally, someone has written a great guide for traveling solo. Dr. Mary Travelbest has a fun book with great tips, suggestions and other ways to make your solo vacation great. This is the kind of book that you will love reading and will probably buy an extra copy for your friends and family members that just love traveling. – Cindy Clark

CONTENTS

1 INTRODUCING 5 STEPS TO SOLO TRAVEL

Introducing the idea of steps of solo travel for women

This travel guide addresses why you should go solo. This section offers

guidance on why traveling is important for your mind, body, and spirit. It is

written for women who, like you, need help with motivation and planning,

equipment, packing, food, maps and attitude. To get started, I'll answer

what you need to know when traveling on your own; which is, without an

organized tour. You'll find millions of women are traveling the world solo

today and will do so tomorrow. These women are confident, streetwise,

and eager to learn more.

Here are four reasons to travel solo or independently (and hundreds more in this book):

1. Get comfortable with yourself.
2. Discover complete freedom.
3. Boost self-confidence.
4. Make connections.

You don't have to negotiate with anyone about where you are going, when to stop and explore, how long to stay, and what to eat. These are a few statements from others explaining why they like traveling solo or independently.

"I travel because I have an interest in the places I go." (Martha P.)

"My appreciation of art and history is not enhanced by company, and I have no expectation to meet people when I travel." (Suzy G.)

A solo traveler writes: *"In Greece, I was invited to people's homes to celebrate my 75th birthday. Would never happen on a tour or if I had a travel mate!" (Angie R.)*

"Learning the steps to solo travel changed my fears into the reality of going. I have been on many of your suggested journeys, starting with Step 1." (Sue R.)

You will love being on your own timetable. You can go wherever you want, whenever you want. You can linger in bed if you are tired from the previous day.

You can decide if you are willing to share a bathroom or not, see exactly what you want to see, and make spontaneous changes to the itinerary. Go someplace close to home or travel far by yourself. Give yourself the opportunity to do it, and to do it confidently.

Would you enjoy never having someone tell you when to get up for breakfast and being able to set your own itinerary? On road trips, it is great to stop when and where you want—to choose to leave somewhere if you are less than thrilled (Lincoln City, Ore), and stay longer if you really like the place (Gold Beach, Ore).

You only have one person to please—YOU!

Over the past 50 years, I have traveled to all 50 US states, and nearly every continent. There has not been any guidebook that was user-focused in my journey. This one is focused on you, the steps to become a best traveler. I struggled with my travels because no one was giving directions on how to become a better traveler and yes, I was lost from the first day. That won't happen to you if you follow decades of experience in these pages. You need some help to keep your feet firmly grounded and your mind ready for what's next. I am honored to share this and other global travels with you, a future traveler. As you read this travel guidebook, you will find both practical how-to tips and mental/emotional coaching. As you travel, observe similarities and differences between yourself and the people in places you visit. The more you reflect on these "oddities," consider the underlying cultural local values. What will you learn about yourself through your journey as you travel through new places? I know your travel dreams can become realities during your lifetime. Don't let your fears keep you inside. There will be a place and a time for you to see the world. Keep your dreams alive by reading and learning how to travel by doing it.

Solo travel can be for anyone, if you DON'T have someone to go with.

Don't let being solo stop you from going.

Dr Travelbest

Take charge of your life with solo travel

Take charge of your life and build your confidence with your solo travel. There are three main kinds of travel: Solo, independent, and tour travel. This book will cover the first two choices, solo and independent. This is not a book about tour travel. This book is for the traveler who wants more than a tour.

Before I became a solo traveler, I was shy and introverted. I did not have confidence in myself. I was often quite lonely and sad, and my life felt unimportant. I was bullied by my so-called friends as a young teen. These so-called friends smeared oil and grease from carbon paper all over my body and mocked me. I was in horror and tears that anyone would do this, especially friends. This has never been publicly shared before, as I was shamed. The experience of travel has lifted this and other mental burdens from my past and now I can share the lessons I have learned throughout this book—of new places to see and favorite places to revisit. This was a transformation for me, and I know it will transform you, irrespective of your age or lifestyle. This is no longer a story about being shy and under confident. Travel has changed my life and it can change yours too.

Positive attitudes travel well

Keep saying "yes."

Face your fear of going alone. Meeting people may be a challenge. Talk about the weather, transportation, or ask a question when you want to start a conversation. Common sense is critical here. Confidence building is like a snowball which gathers momentum and mass as it goes downhill.

When asked if I could name independent travelers who inspire me, here's what I said about my friend Cindy, who retired a few years ago with a lifelong, persistent travel bug—just like me:

She wants to travel while she is still able and willing to go places. Cindy planned a trip to include dozens of countries, many cities, and many outstanding adventures. She knew she could go to the European Union for up to 180 days in a year. She planned the weather strategically, departing the northern countries during the cooler months. She loves the hot weather, so planning was weather related, to be the least cold she can.

She enjoys warm days wherever she finds herself. Cindy inspires me to travel more.

My real-life role travel models were my mom, Dorothy, and my grandma, Dora. My grandparents often went back and forth to Ireland and New York on steamer ships several times a year. The other role model was my dad, from his travel through the Navy and travels to Yuma, Arizona in summers during college. My dad was able to hitchhike across the country several times, from New York City to Yuma. He served in the US Navy in Sydney, Australia and San Diego, California. My mom went to China independently with one other woman, smuggling Bibles there in 1985. My parents traveled together independently to Ireland, Israel, and Canada, and almost moved to the Middle East in 1979. We know women who were influenced by their mothers travel more frequently. This is why I highly encourage mother-daughter travel whenever possible. If you are a daughter, reach out to your mom and see if you can make a trip with her. If you are a mom, let your daughter know you want to travel with her. Give yourselves the gift of travel. Make plans to travel now to somewhere you have always wanted to go. This is the day. Do it now. Don't wait until tomorrow. You can do this. Who inspires you to travel?

How to read this book?

You picked up this book because you want to travel independently, and you need both guidance and inspiration. Every advancing step is one level toward finding meaning for you in travel. The first chapter outlines the five steps and then in detail what they mean. The following chapters in Part A tell you how to travel in each category (packing, hotels, airlines, health, etc.) Part B in the series of five books will be published soon, including the five steps by destination for where you should travel. You can start at Step One, continue through to each level, or move back and forth between levels. Each chapter has a brief outline and summary. Whichever method you employ to read this book, I hope you will find it useful.

Reading Tips:

- ☐ Safety precautions will be seen throughout the book

- ☐ Health is a prerequisite for traveling solo.

- ☐ Planning and reading this book can help protect you from disaster.

Assess your travel needs to find your travel space. Assessing yourself and assessing your specific needs starting in Part One. Part Two details destinations and travel insights to guide your pleasure in travel. There are Q&As, Tips, and Lessons. Here are few samples you will find in this book:

Q&As:

Why is starting a trip so hard sometimes?

Answer: World traveler Anne Morrow Lindbergh said starting a trip is like a snail being pulled off your own personal rock. Once you get started on the journey, it gets better. Are you a snail who needs to be pulled off your rock? As you plan your trip, I hope you feel more and more like the eagle, who soars above and is a travel champion.

For a recently divorced woman, how should I travel?

Answer: Start small and become comfortable. Go local first. Try 10-15 miles from home and make it a regular weekly or monthly adventure.

Increase the distance to 30 miles and then go to the next state and make conversations at these new places. You will gain so much confidence from your travels.

Travel Tips

- Take care and be safe when going out at night. If you can do it in daylight, it's best.

- Learn the maps to your known destinations as best you can before you arrive.

- Keep your passport safe with extra copies elsewhere.

- You want to be confident when you travel so talk to yourself in the mirror to build this trait.

(preview) Chapter 2 Tips on How To Pack:

- Packing takes practice step by step.
- Travel light to save energy and time.
- Pack half of a small suitcase. The other half can be for things to give away or donate.
- Consider a small backpack instead of a suitcase, if possible. The basics: Medications, cosmetics, and one-of-a-kind items.

Lesson Learned Carry a flashlight

At night, it's hard to see in the dark. I have tripped and fallen to the ground which was terrifying in a strange place. If you're tent camping, have a handy flashlight if you need to use the restroom facilities. You can find some which are hands free, too. Keeping a flashlight with batteries or using the flashlight app on your smartphone can save you from tripping or falling.

Best things about solo travel

Travel fights off depression, demands creativity, and improves relationships. Stepping outside our comfort zones, physically and figuratively, challenges us to seek happiness and social stimulation, and offers voyagers a fresh outlook on life. Through the journey, we both help others by building companionship, and develop confidence and inner peace.

My solo travel as a teenager was from my new home in Chicago to New York City, Long Island, and upstate New York for three weeks. This helped build my travel experiences then and through the following decades. Travel is much better than getting "stuff." Stuff is easily replaced and forgotten. Before this solo trip, I had recently lost almost all of my stuff in a moving van accident, so I knew from early teen years that stuff was all temporary. Memories last a lifetime and you will treasure these so much more than stuff. Those three weeks in New York shaped my future desire for travel. I could travel anywhere, and I could do it by myself—so can you.

It can be solo or independent without a "tour guide." Solo travel is for travelers who need both flexibility and convenience. Solo travel refers to self-organized, non-package trips, which can also include unplanned or non-pre-booked activities.

There is a contradiction between the solo traveler and a guide book. What the solo traveler wants is accessibility, authenticity, and consumption of experiences which they value, within a price range which fits their budget. A solo traveler relies on experts to help them plan and enjoy their experience in the best way possible, such as this guidebook.

What can this guidebook do for you? Dr. Travelbest's 5 Steps to Solo Travel can provide you with access to things you are looking for: helpful suggestions and tips on what not to do, how to get more freedom through travel on airlines, hotels and car rentals. I want to help you clarify your goals step by step, achieve them, and reflect upon the real value you receive through travel.

How does freedom relate to travel? Freedom is the motivation for travel in general. Freedom from doubt is what the responsible traveler wants to experience. Freedom from guilt about sustainable travel will be discussed in later chapters.

Where do we learn about freedom and tourism? We learn about it from knowledge of tourism, such as: cultural, economic, geographic, social, and technological. Freedom can be experienced in many ways during travel. Solo travel can be freedom from work and to choose activities outside of your itinerary. It's that break you may need from what you do the rest of your life.

Starting Out

The solo traveler may start out looking at travel brochures for ideas on potential locations and activities to visit. Thereafter, they review more substantial information before and during their vacation, including reading guide books from publishers such as: Lonely Planet, Rick Steves, National Geographic, and Rough Guides. Guidebooks and travel blogs help with cultural knowledge for the solo traveler.

Solo travel is about the experience, all which leads up to going somewhere new, and subsequent events. Books like this one help you decide where to go, how to go, what to see, and how to experience it at the level where you are.

Tours are mostly bound by strict itineraries, packaged experiences, and appeals to the mainstream tourism marketplace. The solo traveler chooses to escape the mass appeal destinations, gaining freedom to choose authentic and non-commercial experiences as they want. Is packaged tourism bad? Of course not. The responsible traveler values authenticity and can find it solo or on a group outing. Authenticity creates experiences integral to local people's traditions, cultures, and rituals, instead of those curated for tourists. This is not necessarily good or bad; it's just different.

Freedom from constraints of travel industry middlemen is seen as an opportunity to engage in organized tours. Some operators may offer a section called "solo" on their website, for people who don't want to book their holiday through a tour operator. You can still choose from a selection of accommodations, day trips, and short overnight excursions. These tours support the locals and the local environment rather than the global tour operators.

For some travelers, freedom is their top priority. However, freedom for any kind of tourist is not a one-size-fits-all. It is within a normal range of acceptable and unacceptable behavior. People want companionship, but maybe not for the entire trip. Solo travel for even a part of your trip can be the solution to your needs.

The word for a wanderer is "**Solivagant.**" It is derived from two Latin words: "Solus," meaning "alone," and "vagans," meaning "wander." It's a noun which translates to "a solitary wanderer." Solivagant, as an adjective, can also be used to describe those who meander in new places alone to experience the wandering adventure.

Solo travel is an important part of worldwide tourism from an economic and cultural viewpoint. The motivations for why people travel and the decisions they make while traveling have been studied through active travelers. There are two elements of independent/solo travel: 1) experiencing an evolving itinerary and 2) willingness to take risks in selecting destinations.

Why should you GO? Why should you keep saying YES?

- Step out of your comfort zone

- Enjoy your life

- Innovate

- Explore

- ⬚ Self-actualize

- ⬚ Pleasure

- ⬚ Emotional experience

It seems that the more places I see and experience, the bigger I realize the world to be. The more I become aware of, the more I realize how relatively little I know of it, how many places I have still to go, how much more there is to learn. Maybe that's enlightenment enough—to know that there is no final resting place of the mind, no moment of smug clarity. Perhaps wisdom, at least for me, means realizing how small I am, and unwise, and how far I have yet to go.

– Anthony Bourdain, travel expert

Facing fears of solo travel

No matter who we are or where we come from, we've all faced the fear of trying new things. Hodophobia is the fear of travel. Oftentimes, it emerges as a fear of means of transportation, like airplanes, especially after many recorded and highly publicized disasters instill fear into the public. Hodophobia creates anxiety, but it can be managed and even surmounted. You can overcome it.

This fear is real for many people—not just women. Physically, fear and

13

anxiety can cause shaking, crying, nausea, headaches, or sweating. The specific fear I want to address is the travel itself, not the fear of being trapped or helpless in a potential public attack (agoraphobia). Hodophobia can be linked to other phobias, such as claustrophobia (the irrational fear of confined spaces), risk aversion (where people tend to prefer outcomes with lower uncertainty) or performance anxiety (fear of doing something in front of people, commonly called "stage fright"). How can you cope with this fear?

Five ways for coping with fear of traveling:

1. Set realistic expectations for yourself. Many people have shared their stories on the internet, most of which are highlights or horror stories. What do you hope to experience for yourself? Why? How will you reach your goals?

2. Use what you learn. The more you learn, the less stress you feel. Say goodbye to hodophobia.

3. Visualize. Imagine yourself navigating city traffic and even detailed experiences such as pulling into the perfect parking spot. Visualize your own success while you build confidence and reduce personal stress.

4. Plan your destination. If you are driving to your destination, sit down with a map and plan how far you will travel each day. Make hotel reservations and note the locations of nearby restaurants. If you are traveling by public carrier—such as a ship or a plane—confirm your bookings a few days before you leave. Allow plenty of time to arrive early and make a backup plan in case of delays. Don't forget about asking for early check in and late check out.

5. Breathe. Your body's reaction to your mind can improve your outlook. Breathe deeply to remind yourself of your current body rhythms.

In the book, *The Gift of Fear*, Gavin de Becker says to trust your gut. Here are some suggestions I learned from trusting my gut:

- Adopt the art of possibility
- Find others who have overcome this same fear
- Find an advocate
- Accept the present
- Be transparent
- Ask yourself if it is really a fear of travel itself, or a fear of changing places

Face your fear of going alone

Meeting people may be a challenge. Common sense is critical here. Building your confidence in meeting people is a skill you can develop; it grows with experience, and probably won't appear overnight. You can have fun on the journey even when things don't always go your way. The weather, for example, may not be what you expected when you originally planned your trip. You may have a minor disaster, order the wrong meal, lose your luggage or you may be sick. Do what you can with what you have! Follow the guidance found in this book.

How to meet other people

"Good company in a journey makes the way seem shorter" (Izaak Walton, 1593-1683).

Wear a smile and ask for the time of day. If others have an accent different than yours (yes, you have an accent), ask them where they are from. Share a common problem, tell a joke, comment on the weather, and ask about a news event. Research an interest, such as pickleball or a musician like Elvis. Go ahead and make appropriate contacts when you arrive.

I've been in the marketing business for many years. Here's what I did to meet new people. I wrote cold letters to advertising agencies in Hong Kong, China and Taiwan, telling them of my upcoming trip. I also called ad agencies and visited the people who worked there. My circle of friends quickly multiplied beyond what I had expected. Be polite and friendly, in hopes they will meet you halfway. And they will.

When you travel solo, people will come to you. They seek you out. They will be happy you were there to talk. Independent travel is for all, especially if you DON'T have someone to go with. Don't let this stop you from going places.

6 tips on solo travel

1. Strangers are just friends you have not yet met, most of the time.

2. Appear to be confident, even if you are not.

3. Be yourself.

4. Learn technology, especially how to read a map.

5. Make meaningful travel experiences.

Common dangers of independent travel

▢ New shoes often lead to blisters

▢ Altitude sickness.

▢ Leaving valuables in your car if you are in a hotel.

▢ Drinking at night and then going home alone in a foreign city.

▢ Swimming alone.

▢ Not keeping your passport and passport copies safe.

▢ Looking like a tourist.

▢ Being a target for a pickpocket.

One of the defining trips in my life was going to Africa for a month, because I was so totally away from my traditional culture and did not speak to anyone who knew me or my background during the trip. There were few Americans on this journey. Being so isolated taught me survival lessons. I was able to build confidence and trust myself during this time. You may not need to go so far, but you can do something which can help you build your confidence. You will be able to feel positive about yourself, even in a small way. This is why I want you to explore, to discover yourself in the process.

Why should you go by yourself? Should you go with a friend instead? Won't you have a better time since you can share this experience with someone else? There's no "right" answer here, but asking these questions will help you understand your own needs.

Lessons learned through Christ

The Bible has an answer in 2nd Corinthians 12:10: *"When I am weak, then I am strong. For my power is made perfect in weakness. Therefore, I will boast all the more gladly about my weaknesses, so that Christ's power may rest upon me."* Our own abilities prove inadequate. However, if you look at this as an opportunity to try something new, you could be pleased with the outcome, as so many others I speak to have been transformed through different forms of travel. My personal weaknesses are seen throughout this book in my lessons. Every one of these weaknesses has been included so that you don't make the same mistakes. Another quote from 2nd Corinthians 5: 16-18 says: *"Old things have passed away; behold they have become new."* Hence, new adventures will replace the old ways. Good luck in your future travels and new experiences, with God as your companion.

The 5 steps for solo travel

What level of traveler are you? Identify the step you currently match, and then consider the' next step you want to reach. You will learn about The 5 Steps to Solo Travel (™) which describes five distinct levels of travel experiences. The steps here will help you learn which kind of traveler you are. You will read about these steps throughout the book; the first steps are oriented towards beginners, and higher steps provide information for more experienced travelers. These steps have been road tested since 1993, with the publication of my first travel guide book for the solo or independent traveler. See Part 2 of this book to navigate destinations for these steps.

What kind of a traveler you think you are may also depend on your health and financial circumstances. This section of the guide will help you find your step and learn more about this type of travel. See yourself on at least one step of the steps of experience, which can change depending on current conditions. Be ready to move up or down to a new step.

The 5 Steps to Solo Adventures

Step One: No experience yet, but ready to start a solo trip. Suggested trips include: starting at a city where you have a family member or friend with whom you can stay. It could be Boston, New York, or even a suburban town in Montana. It should be relatively close to your home state and not for an extended period.

Step Two: Some solo travel, but mostly group travel or organized by tour guides. Suggested trips include: state-to-state travel for an extended period, completely on your own.

Step 3: You have traveled solo to a different state or country. You may have already been to places like Canada, Mexico, Hawaii, or Alaska. Suggested trips might include some of these places, but with a more adventurous or spontaneous spirit.

Step 4: You're already taken several independent trips, but not in a foreign language environment. Whether you've been to Australia, New Zealand, Ireland, the UK, Germany (as most speak English there) or internally within Mexico, here's to your next step out to experience a new local culture.

Step 5: Have been to many different countries where they speak another local language. Have faced challenges like surmounting cultures largely unfamiliar to your own, or navigating travel in a place where transportation is limited. These places are harder to reach, though not unwelcoming--here's to your next step! **Examples: Kenya, Africa or Japan.**

Step One

If you've not been traveling, and you're thinking about starting, this is the place for you to begin. You may have traveled before, but it's been a while—or the entire COVID lockdown has given you no confidence about travel, and you need to jumpstart your engines. There is a special bonus section at the Appendix about COVID and travel, so you can go visit this later for specific needs and safety.

Consider: when you were in kindergarten, you were just starting out, and you knew it. If you realize you are once again just embarking on a new journey, you will give yourself some extra time and grace to travel alone and learn. Ask questions along the way. Don't assume everything is going to go well (it won't!). Accept that plans will go smoothly some of the time; celebrate those moments. When you look back on your personal history, you will be telling the story the way you saw it unfold, so it will be from your perspective alone as a Step One traveler. Don't carry extra baggage from plans that didn't go exactly as you prepared them.

Step One is the first trip to a nearby place in the US. It could be a car trip to a city or town within a few hours' drive. You may set aside one day to drive to a new place and take a walk through a meadow when you get there. Each step you take without a guide, you are growing in independence. Prior to your trip, do your research and use the internet, including social media platforms. While on your journey, talk to people. This is the key point—it's YOUR journey, not someone else's.

There's a lot to be said about having a companion on your trip. Having someone to share the fun with is a good idea for many of us. However, not everyone has someone to travel with. If you are in this situation, the best idea is to start planning a customized, solo trip—just for you. Make your arrangements as if it's just for you, so you have no excuses not to go.

For more of a challenge, take a look at your destination's geography. Invest in a map, read your atlas, and use your smartphone to figure out how to get there. Figure out the best time of day to travel, as well as whether you will be staying overnight. You don't need to book your accommodations, but you can if you want. You may also want to stay with a friend or family member for just a night. You're in Step One! You can do this.

Step Two

The next level adventurer doesn't need to fear strenuous exertion, but is eager to experience a healthy dose of new activities. This step is just one step ahead. Destinations to consider might be in a nearby state in the US or wherever you live—but not too far away. Instead of thinking about staying with a friend or family member, consider a grander adventure, perhaps, by yourself. You are going to wander, explore, and experience new things. Be ready for a slightly different experience from the first step, but without any significant fear of the unknown. Visit a nearby state, just a short flight or a 200-mile car trip away, where you might stay overnight for at least one or two days. After arriving at your destination, you might visit local sites on this trip through public transportation, such as the train, bus, or trolley. If there is a zoo, spend a few hours wandering through it as a nature exploration. Go to a park and walk the perimeter. Find a shopping center and explore some new stores which you have not been to before. Try a new food item (or several!). Explore new tastes, smells, and colorful places to tease your curiosity.

To travel at Step Two, you will need to consider the places you will sleep, eat, and tour, as well as learn some context of the history of the region. Take note of sightseeing suggestions from others. Visit your local AAA office, contact a travel professional, or book your own flight on the airline. You can do this because you are already at Step Two!

Step Three

At this next level, the travel step includes passport-required countries, international visas, and/or driving. Your travel has advanced to the middle point in the 5 Steps to Solo Adventures. Step One was about getting started with a drive to another city. In Step Two, you went to another region or state. You are now at Step Three and you are more accomplished than most travelers, even if you don't realize it. To advance to Step Three, you must have already visited different parts of the USA, various regions within your country, and are now ready to partake in more exploration outside of your small bubble. You don't necessarily need a guide to show you the way. I recommend checking with the CDC and State Department websites before traveling to any Step Three destinations.

As you step out into regions farther from home, it's time to focus on the geography and the climate of these regions as you plan your trip. The timing of your travel will be key to your comfort and enjoyment. Economy also plays a role, making supply and demand a determining factor as well—especially if you don't like being in a crowd. Step Three is for the more advanced traveler, so get ready for some bigger slices of adventurous fun. In Part B, you will learn more about US states such as Hawaii and Alaska, where you don't need a passport. Canada and Mexico are also in this category, but a passport is required. Airline, rail, and ship travel may require certain health passports, vaccinations, or proof of insurance.

At Step Three, you are becoming a more invested traveler, as you are not going to be in a "known place" all through your journey. This step will likely include airline travel, which could be similar to your current region weather-wise, or you may find extremes in temperatures. The climate in Hawaii or the Bahamas, for example, is mild and balmy or tropical. It rains/snows a lot in Alaska, so you'll need weather protection year-round. The items to be focused on are hurricanes and other weather-related temperature and atmosphere changes. If there is a seasonal swing, be sure to review this before you make your final plans, especially if you are solo.

Step Four

Step 4 is the second to last step of Solo Travel. It will be the final step for many readers, and it's a big accomplishment getting here. If you travel to a foreign country, such as Australia, New Zealand, or even Germany, this would be breaking into Step 4. You may be wondering why Germany is on this list. This is because you can travel to many counties in Europe without speaking the local tongue. Most of the people there speak English as a second language. Step 4 is for the solo traveler who wants to explore new countries but is not proficient in the countries' languages. Like Germany, you may discover several European countries which don't require you to speak their local language to travel independently.

You may set a goal for yourself to master Step Four. This is experienced travel. In this stage, you are confident because you have already mastered the art of going places with your own itinerary, even if it's just for part of the trip. You've learned from making your own travel mistakes, and how to recover from them. We've all learned from our lessons and mistakes. It may be hard, but it's not something to complain about. During this training stage, just try not to repeat the same mistakes. Step 4 will still require courage and some planning, but you can plan a more spontaneous trip—perhaps, just a few days ahead, instead of weeks or even months into the future. Step 4 might be a trip to Ireland. Here, you'll be driving on the left side of the road. Most people speak English and have similar customs and heritage with other European countries and America. Gaelic is the traditional language, but most people speak English here. Finding your way around is increasingly fun and full of surprises in Step 4. As for currency, you can count your change and pay with the local currency, by simply doing the conversion in your head or on your smartphone. Step 4 includes these other aspects of staying in foreign countries. Most people speak English. This will allow you to read maps, ride buses and trains and purchase things you need, such as food and shelter easily, though learning some of the local pleasantries "hello," "please," and "thank you" can go a long way in building mutual respect.

Step Five

Step Five is an experienced and fully ready for anything travel champion. You are adopting unique experiences with geography and nature firsthand, even with countries you may not read about in the news or on social media. You will meet people who are different from you. Certain challenges will occur when you visit some countries like China, where you can't read the street signs as different letters are used for language, or when you try to bargain at the market for fruits in Kenya. Step 5 is about going out and having unique experiences in nature, in countries you may not have previously known about their existence, and to see people who are different from you.

I've traveled solo to six continents, and some of these have opened up my mind to new freedoms; for example, in Asia and Africa, I was free to use sign language to communicate basic needs. When I was in my postgraduate studies at Alliant International University, every student had to introduce themselves and the country they were from. I was one of the few students from the USA, and I did not know about many of the countries named, so I went home and looked them up on the globe at night and dreamed of traveling.

If you are heading on a journey which is Step Five, be prepared for freedom surprises, including losing your health, passport, luggage and/or cash. You want to have copies of everything important in a safe place and a backup ready for when you need it. If you are not yet a Step Five traveler, you could combine a Step Five with another step. This way, one part of the trip will include relatively more variety and freedom, while another part of the journey would be more relaxing and restful for you.

The countries I've been to which would be considered Step Five include: Kenya, Thailand, Taiwan, Japan, China, South Korea, and Chile. There are places on our planet today which take a four-day journey to reach, as they are remote. This takes Step Five extreme planning. As an example, my friend Sandra is a scuba diver who goes to remote locations on small islands in the Indian Ocean. This takes weeks and endless hours plus high energy to plan such an extensive trip, usually for several weeks. Be sure you research the regions which most interest you, based on the steps and the itinerary you may choose as a solo traveler.

Chapter One Summary

Chapter One introduces why solo travel is so important to you, the five steps to solo travel adventures and why it has possibilities for you.

The main points of this chapter include:

How travel transforms the solo traveler

What you can expect when you travel solo

Facing real fears of travel and safety

The 5 steps for solo travel, based on experience and ability

This is just the beginning of your adventures. Get ready for your next steps on where you will sleep and what to pack for your trip. If you are already at a higher step, you may skip ahead. You may travel any distance you wish after reading this guide. If you meet the criteria for Step Five—congratulations! You are an inspiration to many who aspire to travel.

2 ACCOMMODATIONS AND PACKING

This chapter is about finding a place to sleep and packing the things you need while you are traveling solo or independently.

Step One

Accommodations

The journey starts with the planning your sleeping

Your trip begins the moment you start planning where to stay overnight. You don't need to wait to get somewhere to have the fun and excitement of a meaningful and responsible trip. You can begin with the research today. Build your confidence and practice of travel, going from Step One and reading all the way up to Step Five.

Setting your expectations for packing will make a big difference. If you are looking for luxury travel, then you will enjoy those comforts. You will also pay a lot for your travel more than someone who is on a camping trip near their home.

Packing

Pack the basics for short trips.

There's not a lot to pack for Step One trips. Essential medicines and phone chargers are important. Be sure you can carry all you bring (hopefully) in one trip. This may be a one-night visit to a nearby friend or relative. You may want to bring a cooler with ice and water, and some nuts, seeds and fruit as snacks. On this trip, you will likely be able to find whatever you need, so try not to panic if you forgot something. You can always buy it or hold off. It's a short trip.

Take your time packing. Don't rush through this early on. Enjoy your minute-by-minute experience as you prepare.

Lesson- Don't Purchase souvenirs on the first day of my trip.

I bought souvenirs all during my trip and had to drag them everywhere I went. It was a mistake. Always shop on your final days if you can, so you can get the most value from your purchases and you won't be carrying them around with you for long.

Lesson- Be able to carry your stuff in one trip.

Don't bring too much. If you can't carry it all in one trip, you have too much stuff. Only bring what you need and leave the rest behind. I've taken too many of the shirts or shoes on my trips before and wished I had left half behind. What you think of 'just in case' may not be needed or can be bought.

Lesson- Forgetting my suitcase on a car trip.

On a three-day car trip with my 1-year-old daughter and husband, we remembered the diaper bag, but forgot the suitcase to bring to the car. We had enough diapers and made sure we washed our own clothes daily on the trip, then put them back on. We were barely able to manage these three days. When we returned home, the suitcase was right where we left it, inside the front room. Don't forget your suitcase.

Step Two

Accommodations.

For the solo traveler in Step Two, you will be staying overnight in an unfamiliar environment for several days. Getting settled in a hotel room or other accommodation requires some preparation, including a credit card to reserve your stay.

Packing

Packing Tips. Travel light to save energy and time. Pack half of a small suitcase. The other half can be for things to give away. Consider a small backpack instead of a suitcase if possible. Pay particular attention to the basics: Medications, cosmetics, and one-of-a-kind items.

Wear a fanny pack. Today's fanny packs come in all shapes and sizes. Some even go under your clothes. I keep my cell phone, earbuds, lip gloss, and credit cards in a small fanny pack. My clothes don't have enough pockets to carry all this, so a fanny pack helps me stay organized and saves time. It may not be the fashion statement you are hoping for, but it can be what you need if you want to stay organized and secure.

Packing your medications. Look for a way to organize your meds, with a daily pill keeper. They come in many sizes and shapes, for example, 7 day, AM/PM and big enough to fit all your pills and vitamins and daily color codes. To keep it simpler, baggies or zip locks can be good, but seal them carefully. Many women are naturally low in iron, and if that's you, be sure to bring your iron pills, as they may be a key part of your meds while traveling. When you fly, keep your meds on your person or in your carry-on, in case your luggage is lost.

Step Three

Accommodations

Sleeping away from the tourists

Stay at an Airbnb or VRBO. If you have used one, you are already experienced. If you have not yet done so, know it's an adventure. Each place is different, so don't expect the same amenities as a hotel.

Some have even nicer amenities, but it all depends on the owner. Whether you choose a hotel or an Airbnb, read Customer (Google, Yelp, or Trip Advisor) Reviews before you book your stay. You can find out so much from what other travelers tell you. If you're staying for just a day, Airbnb may not be worth booking, as they have added so many new fees during the pandemic. However, if you're staying for several days—even a week or more—an Airbnb can be suggested for solo travel. It may feel like home away from home. One tip: You can book one night first, and then try to contact the Airbnb owner directly to see if they can add additional nights and want to book you "off the record books" for an extended stay week at a lower price.

Avoiding "single supplement" fees

A single supplement is a charge paid by a solo traveler to compensate a hotel or cruise line for losses incurred because only one person is staying in a room or cruise ship cabin. Most hotel rooms and ship cabins are built under the assumption at least two people will occupy them. The single supplement is a travel industry premium charged to solo travelers when they take a room alone, mostly for a cruise or hotel stay. The amount involved ranges from 10 to 100 percent of the standard accommodation rate. Some ways to avoid paying this fee include negotiating with the vendor, traveling during slow periods, double up, travel on single tours, cut out the middleman, and travel via adventure tours in places which don't rely on cruises or hotels. You can keep looking until you find the cruise or trip you want without the high price for being solo as an independent woman.

Booking your room

If you are seeking a specific destination, put the city/region name in your computer's browser search engine. You will find several nearby hotel locations and pricing. Look at the map to see where each one is and the cost. The cost is NOT the final fee for hotels and Airbnb's. Additional costs might include services fees, taxes, and cleaning fees. Be prepared for this. A $77 suite could easily cost you $140. My friend Michelle had a bad experience in an Airbnb in Spain that was misleading, false, and unsafe compared to the listed description. She ended up spending six hours resolving the issue. Michelle's bad experience took away from her enjoyment of the trip, and she had to contact the Airbnb owner directly and then the company, sending photos documenting her situation. It brought a very negative experience to the front of her memory of that trip, she said. If you encounter trouble, you can try to work it out like she did, but remember this is not what you want to be doing on your trip, so avoid any properties with negative reviews.

Make sleeping arrangements in advance

Plan ahead of time for flexibility. If you want to know where you're going to be every night of your journey, you can hire someone to make reservations, or you can book yourself for the entire trip. If you love a little bit of uncertainty or flexibility in your plan, you should plan less structure and leave open time. I tend to favor certainty when I'm with a family or group, but when I'm solo, I feel more flexible and prefer to decide once I arrive where the best place is for me. The short window of getting your room settled for day one only could be a good plan for the rest of your trip. For the more experienced long-distance traveler, you will need to consider the value of your time, traveling to and from several destinations or staying in one location. There are advantages to moving around, but the time could keep you from enjoying your trip.

Packing

Save space while Packing your clothes smaller

Rolling your clothes will take up less space than folding them. You can wear your bulky clothes on the plane, including shoes. Shoes in your suitcase can have items stored inside. Neutral colors work best for longer trips, because they will be able to go with any outfit.

Limit your fine jewelry

I take a limited amount of jewelry with me when I travel. First, I don't want to lose it, and I don't want to seem like an easy target for thieves. If you are wearing diamonds, flashy jewelry, or other precious items, you may seem rich to others. It may be best to leave the bauble home and find some new costume jewelry to wear at your destination.

Travel Tip: Store your luggage at a hotel

If you want to store your luggage for the day, go to a chain hotel where you are a member of the loyalty program and ask for the bell captain to store your luggage. They will usually do it for free, which means you can give them a healthy tip, so you don't need to carry it all day. This worked out so well for me in Chicago. I stored it at the Hilton Hotel downtown and was happy to retrieve it later, leaving a tip for the service person.

Step Four

Accommodations

If you are a Step Four traveler, you have already seen your fair share of accommodations and know your way around a city. Since Step 4 is in a region you don't know well (yet!), you may book your full accommodations in advance, or you may decide to only book your first night, and leave the rest unplanned. Have a direct contact with someone at the location, if possible, in case something unforeseen happens. Then, you can let them know you will arrive later than expected, or not at all. Booking through a third-party app, such as Expedia, will limit the conversations you have later on. Managing your own direct reservation will be preferred in order to feel more safe and secure. It may cost a few dollars more to book through the hotel, but in the long run, that could save you stress and cancellation fees later.

Packing

Limit luggage

Packing for Step Four has additional challenges. The advantages of packing organizers or travel compression bags become more valuable, as space is a premium. The best way to pack a smaller suitcase is by using cubes, mentioned below. Many airlines limit your size of carry-on luggage, so find out the exact dimensions and measure your bag accordingly. Seasonally, you will have more clothing during the colder months, so it's even more important to think about layering your clothes. If you have boots, wear them on the plane so you have more room in your suitcase.

Over-packing exercise

Put your suitcase on your floor, fill it with what you need, then remove half of the things inside. You (actually) won't need them. Essentials to keep are medicines, medical devices, water, basic makeup and beauty aids, and lotions you can't find on your travels. Pack one pair of jeans, one pair of shorts or leggings, and one shirt per day. Carry enough underwear and socks for a week. You can always wash your clothes if needed. Looking good vs. enjoying quality travel makes a difference. Limit the number of shoes. My friend Karen had six pairs of shoes in her suitcase for a short trip, and she didn't remember packing them. She ended up with sore feet anyway because the shoes were not high quality. Take only the shoes you really need, not new ones! Make sure they are worn well before your trip.

Packing cubes

Packing cubes are zippered fabric containers, which fit into small spaces. You are not only more organized, but you can also pack more efficiently. I use four nylon cubes. They are the same rectangular shape and size, lightweight and have strong zippers. Although compression bags are a good alternative, your cubes don't need to release air. They are more durable and stack neatly. Plus, there will be fewer creases in your clothes. The advantages of cubes are efficiency, saving space, keeping clothes clean and dry, and preventing you from over packing. The best way to use them is to line up everything you want to bring and figure out how you want to travel. One cube could be for day 2 of your trip, so everything is easy to access. One cube could be your toiletries and electronic cords. One cube could hold a pair of shoes, which you can surround with other smaller items. You'll notice the fabrics; the shapes of your items and the weight will make a difference. Whether you fold or roll tightly, it may take you several tries to get everything into the cubes, but once you do, you're all set for your trip. My cubes fit into a small carry-on bag.

Clean clothes on the road.

Everyone has their own definition of "clean." With clothes, this is no different. My definition of clean is fresh and non-stained clothing, and what really matters is clean undergarments. Keeping the things close to your skin clean will keep you on the road longer. Ensure you have enough underwear for your trip, even if you need to wash/dry them often. Choose fabrics such as polyester which will dry faster.

Here are tips for clean clothes:

- Bring bags to separate clean clothes from dirty clothes.
- Carry detergent with you so you can wash when you have water and air dry them on the road.
- Consider wearing some clothes inside out, for an extra day's wear.
- Wash at night before you sleep, so your clothes will be drier when you wake up.

Lesson learned- Spending too much time making reservations

I spent hours calling our timeshare reservations department planning a trip to Branson, Missouri. When I called to book my designated week there, all of the rooms were taken. I was upset, but I should have been relieved. When I finally arrived in town, all I wanted to stay was one night. So, don't spend too much time looking for your hotel or a place to stay. You'll always find one if you need it, even if you need to drive 20 miles.

Step Five

Accommodations

Book one night

For the Step Five traveler, housing can be difficult, depending on the country you choose. Booking your first night may be helpful for an independent traveler. I did this in several Step Five trips, including a long trip to China.

Lesson learned-Getting to the pool of an Airbnb where I stayed in Bangkok, Thailand was an adventure. I had to borrow the pre-cast plastic fingerprints of the owner on a hook inside my unit to get on the rooftop deck to use the swimming pool. They worked perfectly as if in a James Bond movie with fake fingerprints. I don't think the owners were supposed to have guests, but thanks to the fake fingerprints, we could swim in the pool. It was delightful to relax at the pool as a guest to cool down after a long humid day of travel in Thailand.

You may find some of these non-hotels (Airbnb and VRBO) are better than others. By reading the online ratings from previous guests, you can learn a lot. In Cannes, France, I stayed in a terrible Airbnb, and I left a bad review where I did not feel safe; it was the home of a woman who was a hoarder with a bad attitude. There were boxes floor to ceiling throughout the apartment and a firetrap. Hosts can review you as well, so make sure you're a responsible guest. I've used Airbnb in California and across the USA—in Paris and other cities in France, Madrid, Barcelona, Tokyo, Taipei, Bangkok, and more. You may prefer a hotel for consistent protocols and visible clues of sanitary standards.

What to do when you get stranded?

You could get stranded. Prevention is the best remedy, so here are some tips on what to do if you're stranded. It could be a disaster or an unexpected mishap. Sometimes, things you don't plan for happen. Today's world is hyper connected. If you are in an airport, there is usually a nearby hotel where you can stay. I've slept in airports, when necessary. I slept in the Minute Suites in the Atlanta airport for eight hours. You can opt for an hourly rent on the room. If alone in your car, then you should seek shelter. You don't want to run out of power. Find a place to charge up, recharge your brain, and get to safety. Be sure you drink enough water. If you are hiking, hopefully you have cell service and can call for help. Let someone know you need assistance. Be calm. Consider your resources and situation before you let fear incapacitate you. Be positive and talk to yourself. This challenge is not the end of a potentially life-changing trip. See it as a challenge you can surmount, and be proud of yourself when you do.

Safety when solo traveling

If you're solo, then you're going to be self-reliant, so get used to this and get comfortable with liking your own company. Take yourself on a mental journey. Imagine yourself traveling alone, walking the streets, sitting down at restaurants, and enjoying yourself! Keep your wits about you, and maintain calm, positive thoughts. It's realistic if you practice ahead of time. If you're on the road and in remote areas, there may not be cell service, or your phone battery may have run out. Practice this scenario many times in your mind to get your calm positive thoughts together.

Don't panic. Get into the right frame of mind. Be sure of your options. Perhaps, you can solve the problem by yourself. If not, perhaps, there is someone nearby you can ask for help. You may be able to wait it out, whatever it is. Remember, you do have choices and by reading this book, you will be more prepared.

If you're stranded outdoors when hiking, or your car broke down, that's much different from being in a city without a hotel room or an airport due to an ill-timed snowstorm. If you can't solve it alone, ask for help from a qualified person, but make sure you're safe first. See if there's a passing car who can call for help. If planning for an outdoor trip, you should travel with water and a flashlight, as well as something to keep warm, even a plastic garbage bag to wrap around you if the temperature drops. Be hopeful and responsible. Do what you can to protect yourself.

Packing

Pack like the pro you are. Only include what you need so you don't overpack. In addition to what's already been discussed, add or subtract based on what you can easily purchase where you're going. Small sizes of toiletries can lighten your load considerably. Use a scale to weigh your suitcase and travel bags.

Meaningful travel is not looking like a tourist

You don't want to look like a tourist. If the locals dress in a specific style, such as wearing a sarong, you may want to make a provision to dress like them. Dress respectably for the area you are visiting. If in doubt, ask or research online ahead of time. Looking like a tourist makes you a target for a pickpocket and other traps. My friend Yumi is from Edmonton, Alberta, Canada, and she gave me some advice on this. She went to the Everest Base camp, booking her trip by herself. Her advice to me was to zip up and look confident.

Chapter 2 Summary

Housing and packing both need to be taken seriously, so be sure to plan this to your comfort level. This chapter reviews some of the best practices, including preparing your expectations.

The main points of the chapter include:

What you need to pack for what length of stay

Carry all your luggage in one trip so nothing is left behind

Safe vetted hotels and Airbnb's are at your fingertips

Stay   calm   if   you   are   stranded

3 GROUND TRANSPORTATION

This chapter includes tips on arranging for ground transportation, including getting around on land, ranked by steps of your abilities.

Step One

Road trip preparations

Consider the following if you're going on a road trip:

This checklist includes things to keep in your car.

☐ spare tire with jack

☐ charger for your phone

☐ sunscreen

☐ hat

☐ sunglasses

☐ water and food

☐ blanket

☐ registration

☐ proof of insurance

☐ jacket

☐ wine opener

☐ raincoat or poncho

☐ reflectors

Road trip packing tip: Remember if you bring it, you likely won't need it. If you forget it, you will certainly need it.

Preparing for your road trip with personal technology

Why bring technology with you on your trip? They help make travel a joy. Tech devices, including phones, watches and headsets can be a delight when they work, but when you can't operate them, it's frustrating. What's on your list for "must haves"? Consider your specific needs for day to day as well as the cost of carrying each item with you. We will discuss regular technology as well as some low tech you may consider in tackling ground transportation.

Regular tech: laptop or tablet, smart phone, chargers, portable charging batteries, portable thumb drive, earbuds, headphones, cleaners, headphones, and hearing aids.

Low tech: pen and paper, scissors, stapler, tape, eyeglasses, sunglasses, keys, flashlight, and batteries for flashlight.

Technology preparation begins before you head on your road trip. Research your trip needs in advance. You can use the internet search functions on your phone, laptop, or desktop computer to look up details for your trip. Find out what you might like about the destination and things you plan to avoid. Plan for day one and study the map. Make a list of your favorite places to see, learn about, and eat. Imagine YOU in this destination. Take notes. Which websites should you look at? Trip Advisor, Airbnb, Expedia, and local Chambers of Commerce websites and blogs can be great sources of information. Search the city information office or tourist office. Think of people you know and contact someone from the city ahead of time. Find out if there is a major conference in the city before you travel. What tech tools will you need on this itinerary?

How to stay awake while driving

Combat drowsy driving. First, you should not drive when you're tired, because your brain is impaired. If you must drive, you can keep yourself occupied by talking to someone you love on the phone, hands free. You could sing a song with the windows rolled down. It helps to have more fresh air. I suggest pulling off and taking a rest if you're tired.

Advice-Don't run out of gas

I fill up when my tank is half full, especially when I'm alone on a long road trip. This makes me stretch, use the restroom and take a mental break from a long-distance drive. Plus, the anxiety about running out of gas is not worth it!

Step Two

Traveling with pets

Here is pet travel advice from my friend, Lori, who takes her pets in the car for long distances. She says pets go to the restroom when you do, and they sleep a lot of the time. They make good company for the solo traveler, but even better with another adult on board to care for the pet. Talk to other pet owners for tips on safe travel with pets in the car, on an airplane, ship or train. If you have questions, you can check with your vet or the local humane society.

Van life

What are some of the pros/cons of traveling in a motorhome or van?

Pros: Quick and easy pick up, efficiency, flexibility, and convenience.

Cons: Lack of permanence, hard to get snail mail delivered, no roots, claustrophobia, small spaces, few comforts of home, etc.

Parking a van for the night

You can search the internet for cheap overnight parking. You can also find paid overnight parking near an airport at a good rate. Other ideas: campgrounds, Bureau of Land Management (BLM) lands, hotels, neighborhood streets, casinos, truck stops or Walmart parking lots. Parallel parking is best. Some spots are noisy. The front of the van should be parked facing out. You won't need to back out to maneuver when you are leaving, especially if you are in a hurry. Your cell phone and your keys are the most important things to keep close by.

Motorhome travel has hit a high point across the world. When you visit the Elkhart, Indiana area, where they make 80% of all US Recreational Vehicles (RVs), you will see fields of RVs waiting for finishing. When or if you visit, you'll be dodging a lot of horse and buggy rigs. The Amish and

Mennonites build high quality RVs. This year, there were 426,000 RVs built, many of which were in this region. This growth is predicted to be over 500,000 annually. My personal experiences in RV travel started in the 1970s, with the family trips on the East Coast in and around New York. Later, I RV-traveled from Chicago to North Carolina for a few weeks and later, I spent time in RVs and motorhomes in Las Vegas.

My brother, John, has had an RV for several years and has added many thousands of miles on to the odometer. He's shared some of the best tips and tricks for solo travel in an RV. He considers his vehicle a "stealth van" and he can go unnoticed in nearly any city he chooses. He likes being able to park anywhere in a city—under the radar and unbothered. If you are going on the road, here are essentials to consider bringing: a propane stove, a fire extinguisher and carbon monoxide protector to detect gas leaks. Other essentials may include fan, heater, lights, solar charger, skillet, cutting board, blanket and/or sleeping bag, compost toilet, chairs, awning, solar shower, and table.

Take the auto train to Florida instead of driving

My friends are telling me about the auto train, and it sounds like a great way to travel from the New York area to Florida. You ride in a sleeper car or tiny room and your vehicle is on the train with you. There's room for up to 330 cars on the train, so there's plenty of space. Save yourself the trouble of driving. The train only makes two stops between Virginia and Orlando.

Take care of our planet

Sustainability is for you and me. When you go somewhere, be sure to leave it as you found it. Take only memories from nature. Leave only footprints. Follow the Sierra Club, AAA (Auto Club) and leave our next generations some nature, too.

When I arrive in a new city, should I take one of those 'hop on hop off' buses to show me the famous places?

When it comes to ground transportation, you have choices, depending on your time and budget. The best time to take those hop on hop off buses, where you can watch the city go by from the roof of the bus, is when you have a short time and few other resources. If the weather cooperates, this is better for you to learn about the city, especially if they have recorded audio on board. My favorite cities for watching from the top-level open-air bus include London, Paris, and Barcelona.

Car cooling tips

For travelers and once in a while travelers, if you purchase a new car, try to get one in a light color. This makes a big difference in the heat of summer. In the meantime, here are tips to beat the heat.

- Coat your windows with a sun film, from a professional installer.
- Sunshades reduce the overall temperature inside your vehicle. The traditional reflective models work by pushing away the sun's solar rays and harmful UV rays, while non-reflective shades absorb them.
- Use a reflective sunshade across the front, side, and even back windshield which reflects the UV rays and heat.
- You can turn this around in the winter and use the non-reflective shade side to prevent frost inside your car.
- Park in a shade spot when you can.
- Don't leave your car for too many hours at a time.
- Use a fan you can hold in your hand or on your dash as your car cools down.

Lesson -My gas hog.

My mistakes in being sustainable? Owning a gas guzzler. My first car, a 65 Chevy Wagon, was a huge gas user, and got about 10 miles per gallon. In fact, the gas tank was held on with a chain you could see from the outside.

And once the tank was full, the chain broke. I watched as the entire tank was drained. I was lucky my car had not exploded, and here I watched a tank of gas be drained to the sewer.

Public Transportation: Subways

Take the subway when you are looking to maximize your travel itinerary. It's the fastest, cheapest, and sometimes, most revealing way to learn about the people in a city. If you are in a large city, you will get there faster, and you will experience local people who live there and know their way around. Travel light, so you will be able to move around. Avoid traveling during the rush hours. Recommended subways include: New York City, London, Chicago, Washington, DC., Barcelona, Paris, Shanghai, Hong Kong, Taipei, Bangkok, and San Francisco.

Riding the subway

You've probably seen videos of people jumping over the turnstiles and not paying the fare. Don't let these fool you. You need to pay to ride the subway. Seniors usually get discounted fares. Look this up in advance. Most city subway systems have an app with the map to download. These are easier to track than buses because their stations are permanent and clearly labeled. Oftentimes, subway systems are forgiving. If you forget to get off at your destination, you can get off at the next stop and take the next train back. Some subways—for example, Washington, DC, or Atlanta—allow you to take your bicycle on the subway at no extra cost. This helps with better travel and convenience. For those who just want to quickly get somewhere every now and then, subways are the way to go.

Spin a Globe for perspective

This is a ground transportation suggestion for those at Step Two, who want to get to Step Three. If you don't have a physical globe, find one. Touching the countries and spinning the globe is a powerful planning tool for you as a Step Two traveler. It's one of those objects you will tend to spend time looking at more often than you think. If you love travel or want to travel more, your globe exploration will satisfy your initial curiosity. Another alternative is to get a world map and keep it visible. I had a map of the world printed on the fabric of my jacket. It kept me interested while standing in lines waiting and was a topic of conversation. You can find world maps in many formats and materials.

Step Three

Getting around in your Step Three destination

Your choice of travel depends on the time of year, your resources, and your available time. A good option is snowbird travel, such as a trip to the

Florida coast, Virgin Islands, Scottsdale, Arizona, the Bahamas, or Hawaii for people who live in cold winter climates. Consider if you will walk around the city for most of the time, or if it's a rural or suburban area. How will you get around and how will you stay connected to loved ones?

Consider USA and Canadian National Parks as ground transportation destinations for solo/independent travel. These are welcoming places for visitors of all ages. You will have the tools to explore nature—from seeing animals, to plants, and flowers you may never see in their natural habitat again. Bus transportations may be a welcome option for those who have only traveled by car. There are many options to combine a car and other ground transportation, especially when you are solo and far from home. Research different methods of transportation options and keep flexible, knowing the options for ride sharing vehicles can get you to a depot or bus stop, where you can pick up your alternative transportation.

Working from the road

Working from the road can save you money and lengthen your trip.

If you want to travel solo for several weeks, but your current job only gives you two weeks paid vacation per year, you may have other options. If you are comfortable with working on the go and can use the tools without being in the office, you can adopt a gradual travel approach.

Consider building up your stamina and endurance for longer trips over a period of time. Start with short trips, then advance to longer ones. It also could involve some work from the road if the company is flexible. In our world today, digital nomads are working from anywhere—even while on the road traveling.

During the pandemic, many workers took life on the road. They are road warriors because they are on extended trips, which can even be years long. They are the unseen, the uncounted and sometimes, they can accomplish a lot more than they ever expected. Flexible working conditions keep the travelers going, wherever you are, especially if you are an empty-nester, where your grown children are living elsewhere.

Here are a few careers you can practice on the road:

Teaching online

A lot of people have been teaching or learning online during this shutdown. This type of work requires a strong internet connection and a quiet place, where you can hold live meetings.

Artist

If you have a skill or a craft, you can do this from anywhere. Painters, sculptors, designers, and craftspeople can set up a store on an Internet platform such as ETSY and be in business anytime, anywhere.

Administration

Setting up appointments for others, customer service, troubleshooting, and online concierge are a few admin roles you can do from the road.

Coaching

You can coach from any part of the planet, whether it be for a sport, a career, or even self-improvement classes. Helping others through coaching skills improves your client's strengths and allows them to excel in school, athletics, drama, dance, music, art and more.

Hospitality

Resort workers are often needed, so apply. You could be a ski instructor, tennis pro, or server in the kitchen.

Writer

Write wherever you are.

Sales

Sell services or products online, from wherever you are, especially if you are an outgoing person and have good verbal and written communications skills..

Border crossings in your auto

Are you ready to cross the border into Mexico or Canada but want some guidance? Here are some tools for you to help with timing of crossing, as well as the required lane and identification.

- The U.S. Customs and Border Site offers real-time updates on waits for drivers, commercial vehicles, pedestrian and land ports entry. Use the site to monitor traffic and head to the border when wait times are minimal.
- Take the Ready Lane: select identification—including passport cards, Global Entry cards, and Sentri passes. You may use the Ready Lanes, which are slightly faster than the general lanes. The system works by detecting RFID chips in the cards; standard U.S. passports do not comply.

Step Four

Car rentals and technology

Research your car rental and book (but don't pay) online before you land in your new city. If you're over 25 years old, have a credit card, passport, and own a driver's license, then you can rent a car in most countries. The best way to do this depends on the city you're in and your destination. For example, if you're arriving at an airport, there's usually a shuttle which takes you to the rental car center, where you go to a kiosk or get in a line and finish off your paperwork at the desk. Some rentals have self-service machines, which cuts down the line.

Most rental companies try to upsell customers at the counter, to sell them extra insurance for additional drivers, or to add extra items to the deal. This results in a long queue. For most adults, your existing car insurance will be sufficient, but you should double check your coverage with your insurance company in advance. With car rentals, peace of mind is a top priority. It is likely to be the same location where you also return your car rental. If you want to return it to a different location, the company will charge you extra. I asked about extra fees to drop off a car a thousand miles away, and the fee was an additional $1000. It may be cheapest to return to the same location. If you want extra insurance, you'll pay more. If you don't fill up your gas upon return, you pay. If you don't pay the road tolls or get in any kind of accident, you'll also have paperwork and/or fees to complete after the rental ends. You'll also pay a lot of car rental taxes at the airport. The rental rates are based on supply and demand.

If it's your first time renting a car, ask as many questions as you need, to be secure in your travel. To avoid hidden costs, ask questions about technology, road tolls, and if you will be needing to pay fees. I rented a car, and the location was closed when I returned it, but since this was prearranged, I knew where to leave the keys. Ask if you are returning at a time when they will be closed. Renting a car can also be done through Turo, like Airbnb for autos.

Step Five

Maps and Geography

A map is merely geography in two dimensions. Maps can give insight on natural and man-made features, such as roads, distance, and direction. Topography is the arrangement of the natural and physical features of an area. It's essential for travelers to embrace map reading which includes both geography and topography. Naturally, I'm not a great map reader. I'm not good with directions either. I've had to learn this skill through practice (and making mistakes!) and you can, too. Here are a few tips you can use:

- ☐ Break your route into appropriate legs or segments.
- ☐ Measure your distances accurately, using miles or kilometers consistently, or meters if you're going short distances.
- ☐ Learn to read contour lines and identify key features.
- ☐ First, take time to preview a map before you set out on your journey.
- ☐ Orient yourself with local landmarks.

- ☐ Form a mental map, or cross-reference multiple maps.
- ☐ Refer to a map a lot in the beginning, but don't rely on it completely.
- ☐ Stick to your orientation as best you can.

Don't expect to become a geography expert overnight. Like anything else, you can improve your skills with practice. I'm always getting lost and want to travel more, but I don't want to feel lost which would keep me away from future solo travel.

How can I improve my sense of direction while traveling on the ground?

I suffer from navigation deficiencies, but I'm able to talk myself through hard situations and improve. I can help you think of yourself as a person with proficiency in navigation once you locate landmarks and establish a sense of place. It's never too late to improve your sense of direction. You can start with this goal—to memorize details about physical cues you see and spaces you visit. Practice with physical objects such as Legos™, artworks and historical markers as well as special imagery when you go on a hike in your neighborhood. You can also offer directions to other folks with their navigation, sharpening your own cues as you help others.

Learn a new language while traveling

If you are traveling in a new country where you don't speak the language, and you're already there, you can still be successful as a traveler. Keep a positive attitude, use hand gestures, and give yourself a chance to make mistakes. Here are a few ways to learn a new language quickly:

1. Smile and use facial expressions or gestures more than typical. Learn key words early on: Please, thank you, and the bathroom are important expressions.

2. Use words which are the same in two languages. These are called cognates.

3. Learn a few most frequently used words in the subject to show you are trying.

4. Practice the words with hand signals while looking in the mirror.

5. Use physical tools like flashcards and an offline note taking app.

6. Say words out loud repeatedly, using soft, loud, and normal tones so you get comfortable hearing yourself..

7. Practice daily, like every time you brush your teeth. Make it a habit.

Summary

This chapter provided good ways to get around, to make your trip more successful when you were on the road.

The main points of the chapter include:

How to prepare your car and your personal technology

Why road trips are solo travel friendly

Navigation will be your friend on the open road

Working from the road has potential

Geographical understanding will take you to faraway places with more confidence

4 Air transportation

This chapter is about traveling by airplane.

Online Travel Agencies (OTA) for beginners

As a beginner traveler, be aware of your many travel airline options. You can call to book your ticket, but this may be more costly than online booking. Online is generally less costly for airlines since it is self-service. Online Travel Agencies (OTAs) Expedia and Booking (formerly Priceline) are the main travel agencies. You will read more on them in Step Two. Some airlines are not listed on the travel agencies lists; for example, Southwest Airlines is not included in most of these agency sites, and will accept direct bookings over the phone or online, so independent travelers reading this can look there first. Free online travel pricing services including Skyscanner, and Google Flights are growing in popularity. Shop around and find what flights are best for you. There are other options besides these obvious choices, some of which are subscription-based and charge a fee. After booking, you will have 24 hours to change any of your flight reservations without penalty. Note these rules can change by region, so be flexible.

Airport tech

For Step One airline travel, ensure you check in to your flight online 24 hours ahead of time using the app or website. Print your boarding pass or view it on your phone, and show your government ID so you can pass through the TSA screening to reach your airport gate. There, you will show your boarding pass to your airline representative before boarding the flight. When on the plane, you will need to follow instructions, including those about putting your phone or electronic devices in airplane mode and other safety regulations.

Free travel using travel rewards

Keep track of your travel rewards and points. How many travelers pay attention to those valuable reward points? How many travel reward companies do you belong to? I'm sure I belong to more than 100 of them. Each reward point is worth about one to two pennies, and the pennies do add up if you travel often. There are experts in this free travel using credit card points, but it does take time to earn and use them. Beginners should consider selecting the cheapest flights and not paying memberships for rewards plans until they have more experience. In the next sections, you will read more about ways to earn points and free trips.

Lesson- Get to the airport early

I drove my 16-year-old son and I to the airport for a weeklong trip to Colorado. When we arrived at the airport, his suitcase was not in the car. It was packed, but back at the house. We had enough time to drive there, get it and drive back and still make the flight. Getting to the airport early saves a lot of problems later on.

In flight planning

Pack a small bag for "in flight"

This bag is only for your essential items: headphones, medicines, keys, reading material, phone and charger, documents, blanket and extra socks, underwear, and toothbrush.

Remove worry

Flying can be safer than driving so be confident of your flight and pilot. In Psalm 139, David helps us turn worry to worship. "You search out my path." Remove worry and know you are not alone. The message here for all of us is not to worry about things you can't control. You can convert the concern to a praise event.

Step Two

Airline bookings for more advanced travel

Domestic trips should be booked one to two months in advance. International trips are best planned even further in advance, especially if you are traveling on specific dates or for a holiday period. Those are when flights are highly sought after. Think of economic supply versus demand when it comes to travel. Airline seats are a perishable commodity.

Buying airline tickets from OTA

When buying airline tickets for two people, you may end up paying more. It's best to purchase them one ticket at a time on Online Travel Agencies (OTA). When I only booked for one person, the trip was about $50 less than when I booked for two. The algorithm is set to increase the price as you have more people on the same itinerary. Expedia, Booking and their sub-brands revenues are about $80 billion per year in the US.

Frequent flier miles

Frequent flier miles can get you free trips, but you need to work for them, as the fine print is often confusing. For step one traveler, you can note this. Most airline miles expire after 12-36 months of account inactivity. Unused frequent flier miles can help a nonprofit charity, so consider donating them before they expire. Some have minimums and have made exceptions. American Airlines currently allows you to donate miles, but with restrictions, for example, it must be at least 1000 miles. The program is "Let Good Take Flight." Hawaiian Airlines allows you to donate according to what you wish to donate.

Missing my flights

In Seattle, I slept through my flight and woke up after it had left. I spent the next ten hours in the airport, exploring all the good parts of travel. In Chicago, I was stuck in a cab in traffic on the freeway for far too long and missed my first solo flight to San Diego. If you miss your flight, take the next flight you can. Talk to the gate agent at the airport and try to be patient and kind to others while you go. The journey is part of the adventure and how you handle it makes a difference.

For more entertaining airline flights

Is a deck of cards all you have for your inflight entertainment? If yes, use all of the cards. Make the most of your time by playing a game. If you have a smartphone, download the free Kindle app so you will always have books to read. Learn some card tricks; it may draw people to you!

Check luggage or carry on?

This usually depends on how many pairs of shoes I bring. I'm a fan of bringing only a small personal item on the plane. If in doubt, I'll carry my luggage onboard. However, if I must dress up and bring several pairs of shoes, they don't always fit in a carry-on. The wardrobe changes may require a suitcase. In this case, I check the bag, especially if it's Southwest Airlines. Checked luggage rarely gets lost these days. Still, if you're in a hurry, checked bags can take a long time to retrieve.

Remove food from carry-on luggage

When you go through the X-ray at the airport, it's suggested you remove food from your bag. If you have any food items, you can put them in an easy to access place, so you won't keep the line behind you waiting.

TSA pre-check

To establish TSA pre-check, first complete the online application, which includes payment and creating an in-person appointment for a background check and fingerprinting at an official enrollment center. My appointment was at the San Diego Airport. However, the clerk spelled my name wrong on the card. This requires some explanation when I use it. The fee is currently $100 and lasts for five years. It helps when I return from a foreign country via air, but not on the ground. I don't need to wait in long lines with this distinction when registering with my airline. Not removing my laptop, shoes and light outerwear is also a bonus when going through TSA screening. The pre-check lines are mostly shorter here.

Lessons-Don't spill liquids in an airplane

Spilling my tomato juice all over myself while on a flight was distressing. What an ordeal. I was able to change my clothes and get a new seat cushion, so the rest of the flight went smoothly. I am very grateful to the airline flight attendants.

Step Three
Balancing planning and spur of the moment airline travel

Travel is based on supply and demand as there are limits for certain seats and rooms. Planning travel during holiday periods can be a challenge. Book flights several weeks ahead of your holiday travel. Consider the consequences of loose arrangements. Think about what works best for you in advance. Most of the time, I book airline flights round trip with a return date in mind. However, it may be best to book one way if you need a more flexible arrangement. It can be exciting to be driving across the country—or even another country—and not yet know where you'll be staying for the night.

Here are factors to consider:

- ☐ Holiday
- ☐ Children
- ☐ Language
- ☐ Distance
- ☐ Population
- ☐ Pricing

Best priced airfares

The airfares which offer the best deals are those you can understand and purchase without difficulty as a solo/independent traveler. I have some travel credits available from a frequent travel airline, but when I compare one offer with other offers, it doesn't always provide extra value. I lost out on booking a "free" Alaska Airlines companion fare, which would have cost me $99.00 plus tax. I decided to forego this option as the pricing was too high compared to buying a ticket with another more convenient airline and restrictions on making changes were too complicated.

I prefer to use special booking websites such as Skyscanner. They set up your special price alert with information on changes to the current pricing. I usually check in with an Online Travel Agent before I book directly with an airline to make sure the prices are the best. If the airline pricing goes below your ticketed price, you can request to know the difference and earn a credit or refund.

Three tips for getting the best airfare:

1. Check directly with your airline including any restrictions for making changes.

2. Make sure the ticket is to the right destination and the times fit your needs before you accept it.

3. Cancel within 24 hours if you need to make any changes for a full refund.

Book your flights in sale periods

The best time to book a flight is during a "sale." For example, Southwest

Airlines has many sales, some for 48 hours. Book your flight in late August-December, during non-holiday times if possible. These are generally their slow seasons. Plan several months ahead, if you can. You can save about half of your travel costs through smart planning. Subscribe to marketing emails from your favorite travel companies.

Plan ahead for applying for and renewing your passport

I had to renew passports for some upcoming trip, so I went to the internet and looked up the nearest location. It was at the San Diego Post Office, and my appointment for this was four weeks away. When I got there, it was a terribly humiliating experience, especially since the official said I had the wrong papers and had to make another appointment for four weeks later. I later chose a different location, at the nearby University of California San Diego has a passport office on campus, and anyone could go in and take care of the paperwork with an appointment, and it is much easier to deal with. Many post offices have the forms you will need, but they may not offer the best service. Find out the best place by asking other travelers or searching "Passport Offices."

Plan ahead for duties on purchases

You pay a tax or a duty on goods you purchase when you bring new purchases into a different country. You can purchase some goods "duty-free" in airports—if you follow the rules. You need to inform and pay taxes if you purchase anything substantial. Be prepared.

Plan what you can carry on a plane, for example, nail clippers: Yes or no on a plane?

Yes. You can bring them on a plane, even as a carry on. Razors can be brought on the plane too. This was not the case several years ago, but today, TSA allows it. I've been stopped for bringing nail clippers several times on several flights, so now I try to purchase one at every destination after I arrive. Check the rules as they change. Don't bring any large sharp objects if you fly. For liquids, travel size containers 3.4 ounces or less are currently allowed.

Step Four

Travel rewards

Have you accumulated some travel awards? See where they can take you. Follow travel points experts to get ideas for trips. Keep a running list or a bucket list for which airlines have co-operative relationships for using rewards. Ask the well-traveled people you know for recommendations on where to redeem travel rewards. During holidays, these hotel rooms and airline seats will be limited.

Fly nonstop whenever possible

Take non-stop flights when possible. Always check in for your flights 24 hours in advance. Get to the airport 30 minutes before the airline's suggested time to cut down on stress. During holidays and international travel, that could be two hours before the flight so be prepared to read a travel book like this one while you wait.

Credit cards and airline travel

I don't use an airline credit card these days, but I may in the future. Airline credit cards may not give the best consumer value, especially if there is an annual fee. When you pay for your airline ticket with a credit card, you can receive your credit on this card if your flight is canceled.

I recommend carrying two bank credit cards when you travel, in case one of them stops working for any reason. I prefer Visa over Master Card or American Express. You can get one from any financial institution, or you can get one which is tied to an affinity group—like a sports team. You can also get one from a university as an alum. My main credit card is USAA and my second is Citibank. Some travel cards offer great deals. I used the Alaska Mileage program for a couple of years, but I have dropped it because it became stressful. The "free" companion fare was not competitive compared to other airline pricing at the time. Southwest Airlines has a program and fee which may work for you. Expect to spend several hours trying to use your deal, and consider your time and frustration as well.

Alternative airline checkpoints for travelers

CLEAR, an expedited airport security program, is perhaps the fastest way to get through airport security checkpoints. As of this writing, about 30 airports recognize CLEAR, but it can also be used in concerts and other venues in the future. CLEAR offers identity screening and security clearance using retina scans. The current cost is less than $200 per year per person and subject to change. There are other pricing features, such as bringing your children along with you, depending on their ages. Is it better than the basic TSA Precheck? For some people, yes. For others, the choice is Global Entry which costs a little more than just the TSA clearance and is for international flights. If you travel often and your airport supports it, then CLEAR may work well for you.

How do I apply for an international travel document?

Answer: If you are planning to visit another region, please check with your State Department website. For a passport, some countries require a valid passport to be valid 3-6 months after your departure, and others require a visa. If you are not clear on this, keep asking because the rules for pandemic travel keep changing. If you are a frequent traveler, you can sign up to get alerts about changes. There is no cost to this, called the Smart Travel Enrollment Program.

Language support when landing at the airport in a new country

Vocabulary starters are useful when traveling to foreign countries. Learn the basic words in the language: bathroom, water, hotel, stop/go thank you, please, etc. There are several free language tools you can get from your internet search, and some come with a fee. My advice is to search for the ones you trust, based on previous reputation and cost/value. Some of the "free" apps may make registration so complicated it's not worth your time. Check the reviews before you invest your time. Translation apps I have used and others recommended: Google Translate, Rosetta Stone, Duolingo, LingQ, Babbel, and Busuu.

Watch TV and movies from the country you plan to visit. I watch Spanish language television, for example, and listen to Spanish language radio stations to get prepared for my visits to Spain, Costa Rica and Mexico. I recommend language learning apps. I've used several of them myself to keep up with my Spanish conversational language skills. I like the Duolingo app for practicing Spanish the best.

Lesson-I took the wrong bag

I was in Salt Lake City airport. I checked my ski boots in a gray bag. I picked up my bag and went to my hotel. When I opened the bag, the boots were not mine. All bags look alike at times.

I had someone else's boots, which put both of us on a bad path. I called the airline and we got it sorted out.

Step Five

Tip from a travel pro: General Chuck Yeager

You knew him as the 97-year-old man who broke the sound barrier for land speed. I met Chuck Yeager (RIP Pearl Harbor Day, 2020) on a trip in a first-class commercial airplane sitting next to me en route to the Indy 500 race. Originally, I was booked on the flight the night before, but I was willing to be "bumped" and my upgrade was a First-Class ticket. It turned out to be a special trip meeting and hanging out with Chuck. We joked, had some free drinks, told stories, and had fun from Colorado to Indiana. I asked him if I could ride in the Indy Pace Car, since he was driving it at the big racetrack the next day. He laughed but said no. His tip was to look at the people on the plane and make up stories about where they were going. This is what kept Chuck's mind busy on long flights. You can learn from others on your journey as I did with the man who broke the speed of sound.

Get organized with travel document and TSA credentials

The perfect time to update your credentials is before the documents expire. Get your Real ID, driver's license, passport, and Known Traveler Cards when you can to save time and money. Your state may have special rules on the Real ID. Renew your driver's license before it expires. You should renew your passport six months before it expires. Otherwise, you may not be able to travel to certain countries. The Known Traveler Card called "Global Entry" is a bargain for $100 if you plan to do any global travel in the next five years. Your TSA Pre-Check line will be shorter on every flight you take, which could save you from missing a flight someday.

Summary of Chapter 4:

Chapter 4 is about Air Transportation and how to make the best of your booking and flight experiences. Whether you are new or seasoned, this advice can help you prepare for what's next.

The main points of the chapter include:

Online Travel Agencies don't include all airlines

Carry on your luggage if possible, to avoid delays and lost bags

Know what you can carry on and what you may need handy on plane

Get TSA and Known Traveler identification in advance

Practice using translation tools for the country you are visiting

5 EATING AND DRINKING

This chapter is about eating and drinking on your travels as an independent traveler.

Step One

Fluids are a traveler's best friend. Drink water frequently.

It's hard to go overboard on fluids, especially when it's hot outside. The best fluid to drink is water--clean and fresh. As an alternative, you can take flavored drinks, and soft drinks. Fruits like watermelon or vegetables like cucumbers are great if you need a refreshing liquid. Limit caffeine and alcohol intake if you're outdoors and exercising. Hydration matters. Do you hydrate enough? When you travel, it's especially important to keep your fluids and liquids high, even higher than normal. You are using up the liquids with your exercises, movement, and brain power. So, drink up. Water, juices, or other liquids will improve your life and your skin tone too.

Ask what's in season

Foods that are in season are likely to be most available and freshest. If there is a food item in season, you should consider that choice.

Farmer's Markets

Many cities and regions offer a weekly farmer's market. It's possible that you can visit a farmer's market every day on your trip and therefore get to know the fresh foods, the nearby produce, and the cultural norms of the region, just by walking around and being observant.

Step Two

Eating Vegan or vegetarian while on the road

You can eat vegan or vegetarian food consistently on the road. When you order food, know your needs in advance. Try planning ahead to see what places serve vegan food. You can almost always find staples of beans and rice when you travel away from home. Falafel is another example of a staple you can eat. Vegans I know suggest eating a healthy breakfast, wherever you start out your day. If you need to, carry your own food. Be sure to include a protein source for healthy nutrition, including nuts. Though I'm not vegan, it's a healthy lifestyle, so I'll be more conscious of others who are.

Menus and Eating out

This may be your chance to experiment with a new menu and new items on the menu. Instead of a printed formal folder menu, you may need to use your smartphone to use the virtual menu, with a QR code. Be prepared to pre-order and possibly to pay with your phone, through contactless payments.

Here are tips for eating out:

- Be kind to your servers.
- Ask questions if you don't understand something.
- If you enjoy your meal, tell others.
- Be flexible if your favorite dish is not on the menu.
- Use your smartphone for the menu and the payment (Venmo, Apple Pay, WeChat, etc.) if possible.

Step Three

Refreshment and safety from bacteria

What should you eat or drink when on the road? Don't drink the water in a country you don't know. Drink bottled water only. You can enjoy the finest dining establishments or go for local street food, depending on your appetite and budget. Bread is always a good food to eat, as well as fresh fruits. Before you eat any food, ask your server about ingredients if you have digestive or allergic issues.

Don't rinse your mouth with untreated water

The water may have localized bacteria. Residents have immunity. Don't rinse your mouth or brush your teeth with tap water. Carry a few ounces of water in a small bottle. You don't want to be sick from the local untreated water. Bring tablets to treat your water if there is any question about the content. Beware of all liquids entering your mouth, even in the shower.

Step Four

Extra hydration matters

Do you hydrate enough? I repeat this message about water, because when you don't have your normal daily habits, it's easy to forget to hydrate. Make a conscious effort to drink a lot of water by setting reminders on your phone. Drinking water increases energy. It sharpens your thinking and focus, flushes out toxins and regulates body temperature. So, drink up. Water, juices, or other liquids will improve your life and your skin tone, too.

Groceries and cooking in while on the road

When I visit a new city, my first stop is usually a grocery store or bodega to find out what the cultural tastes are. This can be on the way to anywhere, as you find food stores from road stands to shopping in stores where anything is sold. For Step Four food and drinks, you can stock up for your trip and cook in your Airbnb or snack your meals in your car when you take a break.

Take a cooking class

When traveling, there's no better time to learn a new cooking skill or dish. This is one memory and experience you will take with you. Find out in advance by doing some internet research on "cooking lessons in (name of country)" and you are sure to find some recommendations.

Step Five

Try a new food option

Challenging eating and drinking for independent travelers is the freedom to eat what you want, with the understanding you could be eating something you would normally pass on politely. There will be times when you are hungry on the road, and this is to be expected. You will have more freedom to try new dishes and beverages.

Carry a small container of treated water

You may not be able to find good drinking water quickly, so you should bring a small container of liquids with you.

Ask others when solo eating

If you don't understand the menu, look at what other people are eating. Someone in the kitchen may speak your language. In China, I had to point at what other people were eating and ask for it in sign language. I still don't know what it was, but whatever it was, it was good!

Lesson Learned: Say "No" to hot spicy foods while traveling

When I travel, I've learned the hard way about eating spicy foods: I don't. I've tried to swallow some hot sauce, pizza with hot peppers, chili relleno which is hot and spicy, and other seasonings. I prefer no spice. It may sound boring, but I learned my lesson when my mouth felt that it was burning up. Now I just say "no" which is empowering.

Flavor up your meals

In the US, people are using much more flavor than they used to. This is changing due to immigration from Asia and Latin America. For others, spices can be a way to broaden your global horizons.

Food Poisoning

I ate Udom with shrimp in the 1221 Restaurant near the Taroko Gorge in Taiwan and was awfully sick for a full night—the full bucket experience you don't want to ever have. Don't eat shellfish if you have any doubts about the food. This was a fancy restaurant, but we were in a hurry, so they did not cook the food all the way through. Street vendors may be good since they may be here for many years and know better than a "restaurant."

Summary

Eating and drinking on the road will be memorable because of the smells, tastes and how it is served in different parts of the world. Embrace the differences and eat like a local.

The main points of the chapter include:

Don't forget to hydrate and drink safe water

Eat healthy choices and amounts to sustain your energy

Menus may differ depending on the country, season and weather

Travel allows for new spices and flavors, some of which you will love

6 PERSONAL HEALTH AND SAFETY

Healthy travels are important. Staying healthy on the road will enable you to enjoy your journey. I am a doctor, but not a health doctor, so this advice is not a medical grade prescription.

Step One

Know your physical abilities and your limitations

You would not run a marathon without practicing a few miles each day of jogging. You should practice your travel training with physical activity like an expert exercise trainer would suggest.

Tracking your steps

I track my steps and use the pedometer app on my phone. It tells me how many steps I take, and provides visible badges when I complete streaks. There are monthly challenges, too. Keep track of your mileage. I also use a Fitbit to tell me if I'm moving around. These are reminders I need to exercise and keep track of milestones.

Exercises for sitting down

Here are ten stretches you can do while seated:

Head nods, neck tilts, shoulder shrugs, shoulder rolls, side stretches, spine twists, hip flexor knee lifts, hamstring stretch, ankle rolls, and upper body stretches. Do these in a car, airplane, bus, or while waiting for your next destination.

Sustainable travel for a healthy planet

Sustainable travel is for all of us and our future generations. When you travel somewhere, be sure to leave it as you found it. Take only memories from nature. Leave only footprints so you and generations to follow can continue to enjoy the planet for longer.

Here are some sustainable tips:

- ⬜ Eat and shop local
- ⬜ Take shorter trips closer to home
- ⬜ Travel on public transportation

- ☐ Pack light and smart
- ☐ Travel slow
- ☐ Make fewer flight connections

Special Abilities Travel

This section is to recognize those with special abilities. If you are non-disabled, consider others who are. One can be disabled in many different ways, including mobility, vision, hearing, cognition, and more. The American Disabilities (ADA) Act - 1990 changed some things, but not all. It helps eliminate discrimination, give the right accommodations, and encourages integration. Up to nineteen percent of the US population is disabled, so it's a large slice of the USA. Some people look at disability as inferiority, but this is not exactly true. They don't want to be different, they just are. We need to remove these stereotypes from our travel experiences. Here are some ideas for making a change:

- ☐ Embrace the differences between what is expected and what actually is.
- ☐ Know which biases can be informed by misinformation. Be inclusive whenever you can.
- ☐ Give someone with different abilities than you some extra space and time.
- ☐ Make sure there are written instructions.
- ☐ Turn down fluorescent lights.

Do you know someone who needs more ability to travel? Ask them what they need and listen to them.

Broken fingernails

These may not seem like a big deal to some people but breaking a nail can be a real challenge. I've suffered this many times, so here's my lesson for you. I've had bruises, bleeding, and infection. You don't want this. If you have acrylic or fake nails, you should try to go to a salon and get it repaired, of course. I had a broken fingernail and had to cut it down so it would not be infected later. The lesson was to clip my nails short before I left for my trip. I had to do the regular maintenance to keep them looking good. Keep fingernails short if you plan to travel.

https://www.healthline.com/health/how-to-fix-a-broken-nail

Step Two

Getting overwhelmed when I travel

I have become overwhelmed at times during travel. I have needed to lower my stress steps from the high peaks. Here's what I did to help cut the stress. I whispered quietly about my emotions. I talked myself out of things that bothered me. Then I recovered quickly when stress was removed. This felt like relief, which was empowering. Keeping the tension step low helped me control my body, lowered my blood pressure, let me think clearer, and maintain good physical health.

Self-defense for women

One of the themes for independent women in their prime years is self-defense. My friend Jackie was asking me about this recently. Self-defense exists on many steps. First, don't put yourself in a situation where you will need help. Don't go out alone at night during long trips. Most criminals are not awake at 6 a.m. when I'm out for a walk.

Here's a tactic for defending yourself, just to keep you more aware of your body. Take a martial arts class if you can and learn a few moves. Even if you never get to practice them, you'll have learned some wisdom and strength. Some types of martial arts include karate, judo, taekwondo, Jiu jitsu and many others.

These items may not be allowed on a plane, but you could consider the use when on the ground. Other deterrents against an attack could be a mace or a taser, stun gun, pepper spray, pepper gel, pens, air pistol, keychain and lipstick alarms. Before going out to buy one of these devices, find out if they are legal in the areas you will be visiting. Don't just carry them; understand how to operate and use the device.

What do I do when I am sick while traveling?

Be careful about the food and beverages in regions you are visiting. Purified water may be required, so check ahead of time. In case of sickness, be proactive.

- ☐ Skip strenuous activities.
- ☐ Take a long, hot bath or shower.
- ☐ Eat foods which are gentle on your stomach.
- ☐ Drink lots and lots of water, juice, and tea.
- ☐ Staying healthy is one of the most important things to do when you travel independently.

Mosquitos

In the summer, these pests are more than just a pain. In some regions, you may have allergic reactions to bites. What can you do to stay bite free? Here's a list of things: Stay indoors at sunset when they are hungry. Use Deet and Neet and other topical sprays. Consider B1 vitamins, long sleeves, and pants, as well as sleeping nets. You could get a hat with a net covering your face. Does the country you are visiting have Malaria? Be sure to get vaccine shots well in advance. This information can be attained by contacting the Department of State. Consider asking the locals what they use for prevention and relief from pests.

Skin Cancer

Sunscreen is vital to protect your skin.

Be sure you have the following items if you're in the sun:

- Hat
- Lotion
- Sunburn coverage
- Sunscreen Clothing
- Wear sunscreen, even under your clothing. It needs to have a UV of 30 SPF (Sun Protection Factor) or higher to count as sun protective clothing.
- Light and Muted colors reflect the sun's rays best.
- Color, construction, content, fit, UFP, coverage and activity also matter. For example, if you are wet, the fabric does not protect as much when it's dry.

Environmental hazards

Poison ivy rash is an allergic contact dermatitis caused from an oily resin named urushiol, found in the leaves, stems and roots of poison ivy, poison oak and poison sumac. Because it's sticky, it easily attaches to skin, clothing, tools, equipment, and pet fur.

I had a bad case of this. I hiked in Arkansas; 48 hours later, my neck was full of red clusters, and I thought it was a heat rash. By the next morning, I had terrible rashes all over my chest and back. I also think I had an allergic reaction which was unhealthy. The next time I went hiking, I wore long sleeves, long pants, tucked my pants into my boots and made certain not to touch anything which looked like poison ivy.

Climate Change and Global Travel

You can consider how you travel and cut down on the impact you make on the planet. Using public transportation will cut down your carbon footprint.

My carbon offset is my backyard garden: I've been growing vegetables on a regular basis since 2008. As of now, my backyard grass has been converted to a year-round vegetable farm. I'm growing something tasty to share with those who would like it. Do you have a carbon offset? Let me know about it. Becoming a responsible traveler takes some practice, but it's worth the effort. Solo/independent travelers have a good opportunity to do this, because you're already seeking liberation from group travel and mass appeal activities. You have the freedom to experience authenticity and create your own more sustainable experience.

For airline travelers, consider driving instead of flying to reduce your carbon footprint, especially on shorter trips. Nonstop flights produce fewer emissions. Go economy class to cut your footprint further. Offset your carbon emissions.

For automobile travel, try to take more public transportation, carpool, rideshare, or walk when possible. Fewer cars mean less traffic and fewer idling engines. Avoid unnecessary braking and acceleration. Consistent calm driving can save you, the driver, and your carbon usage. Use your vehicle's cruise control on longer trips and combine errands for fewer overall trips. Keep your tires properly inflated and maintain your vehicle service, such as oil changes. Consider buying a hybrid or electric vehicle.

Step Three

Rest

How can you get some rest on my vacation while keeping my sense of exploration?

We love to explore new places and learn about other cultures, but one day in seven we need to rest and recover. Taking a break can stimulate parts of your brain. Rests refresh. The present is not perfect, so let this be and take a rest so you can get a pause and then return to travel with a new attitude. Here are 3 Tips for being restful.

1. Close your eyes and your brain for longer and longer segments of time. If you have no time, then do it while you are between other activities.

2. Breathe deep and fully exhale while you are lying down for a minute or longer.

3. Schedule on your calendar some time for a nap and get the sleep you need at night to fully recharge your cells.

4. Sometimes you need a total recovery day if you're feeling entirely spent. Rest days are an in-between zone where you can still get moving in moderation. Light exercise, like gentle yoga, walking, swimming, or stretching, are all good choices for the quickest recovery during a rest day.

Prevent Blood Clots.

If you have or think you may have blood clots, you should see your doctor for advice. Here are some helpful suggestions which are good, even if you don't have blood clots. Get up and walk around often when you travel by car or train. On a plane, be sure to stretch your muscles, get up and walk around every few hours, and hydrate. Consider wearing compression stockings.

Exercise Preparation for Travel

What is my normal travel exercise? I try to visit the gym or a workout studio two to three times a week and during summers, swim often, wherever I could find a pool or ocean. I bike, walk, run, or do basic exercises every day. To be a good traveler, especially independent, you need to stay fit.

Here are three medical-related reasons to exercise and stay fit in body and mind:

1.   Exercise is a way of life. It is about moving one's body in ways which help it to maintain and to sustain, even at home. I had osteopenia and then osteoporosis, which are common for women. I am still tracking these bone density factors and be sure to do weight bearing exercises so I can be proactive about my bone health for the future. Make preventative health part of your routine. Your life will be extended so you can travel more.

2.   Mental health on the journey begins with a traveler's attitude checkup. There's a lot we can learn from someone's attitude, so be sure to adjust your mental state if it's not where it should be. You know yourself better than anyone else. If you are open to learning, the mental health checkup starts on a good note. Be sure you have the right attitude when you travel, and check with a mental health professional for more information.

3.   Your heart and blood pressure (BP) should be stable, so review with your medical professional. Before you engage in any new exercise program, you should consult with a qualified trusted person who knows your health conditions. Today's telemedicine allows us to do this from anywhere. My minimal travel exercise program includes squats, lunges, stretches, crunches, and pushups. To give it an extra push, I would include planks, weights, and core strength exercises.

Try out several new ideas on each trip and see how you adapt. The changes are strengthening your neuroplasticity, which is the brain's ability to make changes in structure and function and adapt to these changes. Your brain is actively solving problems on your trip and during your travels. This fosters building muscles in your brain in a new way. With the spice of variety, you will not be bored by your regular activities which are ongoing no matter where you are, such as brushing your teeth, eating meals, and exercising.

Staying connected

Staying connected to loved ones, banking, friends, social media, and news is important. What does it mean to stay connected? While you are planning to travel, you will want to be connected to others whenever you want to be. This includes your family, finances, friends, and your medical information, should this be needed.

Staying connected is about setting expectations for yourself and for others as well. If you are the kind of traveler who only wants to check in occasionally, let your loved ones know in advance. Tell them you love them, but this trip is about a new experience and when you return you will be more available and willing to share. Others may be wanting a daily call home to let others know they are ok.

Finances: If you have a credit card, or cards, did you inform your banking institution when you will be away? Even if you've not traveled far, they could be suspicious of unusual activity on your account and try to reach you. Be sure you respond to their contact, so you won't have your cards de-activated and ruin your travel planning on the road.

Friends: Your friends know you will reach out to them when you can. This is your time to go, so make sure while you are gone, you get the respect you wish for by setting the proper boundaries with friends. You will be glad you did this in advance. Consider changing your outgoing email message to alert you will not be responding.

Medical information: Keep your doctor's office numbers and names handy when you travel, because you may need to get medications while on the road. In the event of illness, you should reach out to your provider, your insurance company and your Telehealth as needed. Telehealth is now more popular than ever. If you have not used this, traveling could be the first convenient opportunity for you.

Slow travel. It's better to see one place and linger there a while than to spread yourself too thin, "like not enough butter over too much bread." You may not remember what you see in so many places. Slow travel can be the best travel; so, enjoy every moment of the planning too.

When I am lonely, what should I do on the road?

If you travel solo, there are times you will feel alone, but you can lean into these times and think of something positive about being solo. For example, you can go at your own pace, use uninterrupted time to daydream, and sleep in if you want. However, it's always good to have a friend you can check in with from the road, just to call and say "hello" to someone you love. Keep the loved ones informed about your location and have a positive attitude so they don't worry. One place you may be able to have a conversation is at the local grocery store. People there are all shopping. Consider asking a question about a food item to break the ice.

Time management for travelers

Be present when you are somewhere and enjoy it. Don't try to be elsewhere. You will be more focused and have a better trip. You can work while on the road, and a little planning ahead can save a lot of troubles later. If you are working on projects while traveling, try to figure out the best time of day for you to be working, so you don't feel like you are working all day long. Depending on your work, you can fit in both your travel adventures and your projects.

Spend time by yourself in reflection

This book is about your solo travel, and mostly not with a guide. Maybe your travel is with a friend or with a spouse, or on a partially guided tour. Either solo or with a pal, be sure to spend some real quality time with just you alone. Carve it out of your "free" time and just take a few moments to spend with your thoughts, your mind, and your heart. Find out what you really want to do and do it. Spending time by yourself in reflection will prepare you, relax you, and give you energy to do things with others in the days ahead. Introspection helps with outward expression. Always remember this. To tolerate others, you must first learn to tolerate yourself.

Phone battery settings

Check your battery settings and find out how your mobile phone activity is affecting your battery health. Of all the apps on my phone, zoom uses up my battery life the most. Find out the maximum capacity, peak performance capability, and optimized battery charging. Charging pattern affects the battery life of your iPhone or other device. To reduce battery aging, the device learns from your daily charging routine. It predicts when your phone will be connected to a charger for an extended period of time. During this period, it turns on the optimized battery charging, which improves the lifespan of your battery. Sometimes, you may notice your phone does not charge beyond 80%. Not to worry! This is a protective mechanism to reduce the wear on your battery. This section is important because your personal health and safety may depend on your device battery.

Stay connected through technology

Even though we want to be independent travelers, we still want to be able to contact others if we have an emergency. Do you have a list of phone numbers and addresses with you just in case you are unable to contact someone with your own cell phone? I've been in situations where I was stuck and could only remember a few numbers to call. Most of our contact phone numbers are already in our phone so we don't rely on keeping a handwritten address book.

Do you have a tablet or a laptop? You can visit an internet café, but those are almost obsolete since most people carry tech in their pocket and are always connected to some device. Check where you're staying to see if they have Wi-Fi. Cruise ships generally charge extra for this service, which can be expensive if you use it a lot. Today you can use Voice over Internet Protocol, VOIP, in the form of Skype, WhatsApp, Google voice, Zoom, Facetime, Line, We Chat, and many more platforms that don't charge a fee, even for long distance and video.

I don't recommend purchasing a prepaid calling card. Most major phone companies offer a plan for international calling so be sure to check. Some telephone services will allow you to pay a daily fee, i.e., International Day Pass, when you use your phone, for example, $10. per day—and only when you use it. Ask your carrier (i.e., AT&T, T-Mobile, Verizon, etc.) first before you go. It may depend on the country, how long you are traveling and your current phone plan. You can also send a postcard or letter to keep in touch from anywhere around the planet. Buy your stamps from the tourist shops or local post office.

Connect by staying ahead with local news

Read a local newspaper or online news local service about where you're going next. Here are three reasons to read a local news source.

1.   You get to learn if there are any special events happening you would not want to miss.

2.   You can find out if there will be an expected crowd or a traffic alert which could prevent you from enjoying your activity.

3.   You will be able to start conversations with locals about things which are going on in the locale because you are informed.

Maintaining connections on social media.

Should you be careful sharing about your travels on social media? What should you be careful about for the content you post and your replies? Social media is a blessing today, but for some it can be a curse. Here are some tips for using it while on the road.

▪ Social media distracts you from the real experience, so consider those you could be talking with instead of trying to get the best social post to strangers. Once you hit the road, limit your social media to when you really need to connect. Otherwise, take a break! You can catch up later. Be where you are. Be in the present. Wait to post on social media until you get home. You don't want the wrong people to know you're away, because your home could become a target for burglars. Be aware when your home address is available to anyone.

▪ Give yourself a time limit daily for how long you will be online. You may need your devices for directions and run out of power, so limit yourself.

▢ Don't share photos of people you don't know unless you have their permission. Consider the privacy of others when you post. And don't embarrass others. Use the Golden Rule. "Do unto others as you would have them do unto you" also works for social media.

Emotional toll of travel

Stress can become distress easily. Distress is what you want to avoid, right?

First, take a deep breath and practice your breathing. Once you have your own body in check, you can move on to the rest of the travel changes. Keep your eye on your phone and your wallet.

Don't be afraid. There are other people in a new place just like you, in a new place and they are not scared, so you don't need to be. Stop worrying. Worrying will not help get you anywhere.

Preparation cuts stress to a minimum. Lay out your clothes for the next day. Have a bedtime routine, even on your travel days. Keep a journal. Smile. Sing. Dance. Move. All these will help reduce stress and reduce the distress to nothing.

Safety and talking about politics while traveling

What is your advice in terms of talking about your political views while traveling in other countries? Should I be outspoken or shy away from expressing my politics?

My advice is to keep quiet. You are a guest. Act like one. Be respectful. You can disagree with the policies, but it's not your place to bring your culture there. You only have to experience their culture. I may not always get this right myself, but this is what I think is best practice.

If one is asked about US politics, you can answer, but stick to the facts.

One example of this was on my first solo trip to mainland China. A newly made Chinese friend asked about my opinions on the USA President, then the president was Reagan. The people in China had limited news and were curious.

Avoid Alcohol and Drugs

Avoid alcohol and drugs while you travel. At the least, take them in moderation when on the road. This is for your own safety. Yes, you can step out of your comfort zone and enjoy life. Create your own personal pleasure and face your fears of going alone. Build your independence. Face your fears and build inner strength, don't go looking for alcohol and drug related problems. There will be other problems on your journey: health problems, delays from automobile traffic, oversleeping, money problems, and other unexpected events. Identifying these kinds of problems in advance is helpful in developing your skill of personal responsibilities and adaptabilities, according to experts in travel education.

Lesson- Tar on my skin from swimming

Santa Barbara, California beaches are great but getting tar on your skin and in your hair is not. I need to rid my skin of these with goop or rubbing alcohol or other "Dawn" dishwashing detergent.

Advice-Limited mobility

Check with the destination to find out if they have access for those with limits on the physical needs of travelers. Let them know you're coming and need extra support. They will likely go out of their way to assist when you give them this heads up notice.

Advice-Sun Rash can go south fast

Protect your skin from Sun Rash and Heat Rash. If you are not used to being in the sun, adjust your timetable. Go out in the early and late hours of the day and stay indoors mid-day. When I visit there, it's often more than 100 degrees Fahrenheit. Sleep or siesta in the midday for your best health. Heat rash is a dangerous side effect.

How can I feel safe when I travel to a new place?

Start at the first step and work toward higher steps. Step one is for beginners and if this is you, start there. Expect to practice and get more experience at the step where you are before you step into the next stage of travel. If you don't feel safe, your trip won't be what you expect, so follow good guidance and prepare ahead of time.

Lesson-Don't get seasick

I've been seasick many times, so here's some of my tips.

Take a Dramamine 30 minutes before boarding the boat. Stay above deck and look at the horizon. Wear wristbands which can prevent seasickness and nausea. Consider what is in your stomach, so don't eat a big meal before you board.

Give wildlife their space

Wildlife can be dangerous, especially the animals. If you are seeing wildlife which is too close for comfort, step back. Leave what you're doing and get away. There will always be another chance to get close with a beast, bird, or insect. No selfie with an animal is worth dying over.

Step Four

What is medical tourism, and should I consider it?

Medical tourism involves people traveling across international boundaries for their healthcare and health needs. It affords you the required medical treatment at a good price. With detailed planning, you can save a lot of money while getting the treatment you need. Before you opt for medical tourism, do your research. Consult your doctor and ensure you understand the procedure. Medical tourism is popular in countries like Thailand, India, Costa Rica, and Mexico. There are packages which include insurance for a selection of treatments, travel, and doctors. Some of the reasons for these visits include cancer, mental health, orthopedics (bones and joints), cardiology, cosmetic surgery, dental—and even wellness tourism, which entails visiting spas, homeopathy treatment (this is alternative medicine, based on the belief the body can heal itself) or traditional therapies.

Think about the quality and the step of satisfaction which you expect if you are going to plan such a visit, and include interpreters, as well as recovery if necessary. There are three steps: the pre, during and post medical consideration. With today's technology and transparency, there is potential for this innovation to grow beyond what it is in the nearest future.

Watch out for snakes

Rattlesnakes can be heard before you see them, so if you are in an area where you think there could be snakes, take out your ear pods and listen. Rattlesnakes use their rattle to chase off prey or warn aggressors. This is your cue to back off. Snake bites can be harmful and even fatal.

Rattles are a defense mechanism for when they fear danger and you should take note and step back. There are more than 3600 kinds of snakes, so be aware of the ones which are deadly or harmful.

Lesson-Don't run out of water

No matter where you are, desert or ocean, don't run out of drinking water. This is one of the most precious resources we need on the road. When you travel, you need to hydrate more often than normal. Your brain needs water to survive so be sure you have enough clean and drinkable water. I've run out of water so many times. I don't want you to go through this problem. Be prepared.

Step Five

How is sulfur good for skin as I travel?

Hydrogen sulfide smells like rotten eggs. You may call it, "The Hot Springs Smell," and it is good for humans because it's natural. Not all hot springs have the same sulfur content. There may be some springs that don't have the smell. Soaking in hot springs can cleanse your skin and remove toxins.

Sulfur helps dry out the surface of your skin to help absorb excess oil (sebum) which may contribute to acne breakouts. It also dries out dead skin cells to help unclog your pores and softens rough or dry skins. However, it is important to note this pleasure has its side effects and cautions. It is not recommended for pregnant women, individuals with high blood pressure and people on blood thinning medications. Ensure you're clear to indulge in hot springs containing sulfur. If at any point you notice a strange reaction, seek professional help. It's always important to stay safe while having fun!

There are different varieties of sulfur, including green sulfur, white sulfur, and iron sulfur.

- Taiwan Hot Springs, Beitou was once the largest hot springs spa in Asia.
- Hokkaido, Japan's most popular spa town Hell Valley, black sulfur waters provide minerals to thermal bathers.

Trouble on the road

If you run into "trouble" like a strike, police in the streets, angry mobs, what should you do? You may have been visiting a city with unrest, angry mobs, and even riots. If you run into situations where you feel it is not your best destination, leave as soon as possible. Move to a new location, even if you need to quickly shelter away for a few hours until things get quiet again. Let the people back home know you're okay and you will reach out to them again soon.

Learn about what is safe by asking local people you meet, checking the local news media, block captain, or neighborhood app. Check your social media using hashtags of the city or region and see what you can learn. Call your embassy, a local official or police department and ask questions about any potentially unsafe situation.

For your safety, here are three quick tips:

1. Get away.
2. Ask an expert for their advice.
3. Contact home to tell them you're okay and stay in touch.

The best way to stay out of trouble in an uprising.

If you run into "trouble" like a strike, police in the streets, angry shouting mobs, steer clear of this type of trouble. As a traveler, you're not prepared for this, so stay out of it. There is going to be unrest somewhere you go, sometime, but if you expect any trouble, get as far away as you can, and quickly, too. As an outsider, you're not prepared to deal with the cause or the results. Stay away and be safe. You want to stay aware of this by listening to local radio and reading about the news in the area. Overall, be prepared for unexpected delays and have a plan to guarantee your safety.

Chapter 6 Summary

This chapter was all about staying safe and healthy while you are traveling. Tips for safe travel include self-defense, safe social media, and avoiding places where there is civil unrest.

The main points of the chapter include:

Know your physical abilities and your limitations

Consider about the possible cautions to take based on your destination

Rest when needed

Personal safety for you

Common sense goes far with a traveler who is solo

7 PLANNING TIPS

This chapter contains general planning tips for the solo traveler which you haven't considered so far. You can travel nearby or far away but there are always trade-offs to balance. Read and practice tips you will need for your journey. You can learn from others, including women just like you. Here are some personal tips, about you as a woman and how you can be your best at traveling in many ways. Not all suggestions will apply to all your trips, but there are many circumstances where you can gain advantage, so select those which work for you.

Planning solo travel trade-off factors to balance

- Bargains vs. Spending
- Easy-to-find directions vs. off the beaten path
- Offbeat vibe vs. regular expectations
- Extreme conditions vs. stable and expected
- Natural beauty vs. urban setting

⬚   Standing invitations vs. intensive planning

⬚   Eat to live vs. live to eat on the road

Step One

This is about travel planning tips for the solo traveler. On your trip, be present with yourself first, and then get to know your surroundings. Get to know your rhythms, keep a journal, breathe, and stretch yourself every day. Look at color. Smell the food before you eat. Inhale everything slowly and smile, which will make you more relaxed physically and show others your confidence.

Photography

If you have a smartphone, you're a digital photographer. Everyone has the power to take great photos. Creating memories is about choosing the best subjects for your photos. Becoming an advanced digital photographer requires special skills, including creativity, patience, concentration, attention to detail, and a few basic technical skills. Consider the purpose of your digital photos. Are they for a special purpose or just for you to enjoy? Are they to share and show to others? Do you just want to remember the moment for you and you alone?

Photography tips: If you plan to use your digital camera, make sure you have plenty of battery life on your camera and storage device, as photos and video take up your battery juice. Check your settings for memory, too. You don't want to run out of space fast, especially with video storage. Consider lighting. The camera can only take images of what it can see, so if the lighting is low, you will not get high contrast. Today's phones take better photos than you could have imagined five years ago. The best photographers know more about the camera, the lens, light and exposure, and workflow for after the image is captured. Think about how you will organize and store your photos and if you wish, use computer software to make your photos look their best. Keep in mind technology upgrades quickly in the digital world. Post pandemic and due to health concerns, it may not be appropriate for you to ask a stranger to take your photo with your camera, even if this was normal in the past.

Fortunately, selfies (self-portrait photographs) were invented as a do-it-yourself rescue. You can learn the art of taking a selfie if you don't know already. Check the shadows, the background, the angle, the lighting—and of course, your confidence! Confidence is one of the best makeovers. Everything looks better with a touch of confidence. You should also wear an authentic smile which makes your face "pop." The best smiles are natural; they are not forced or creepy. Another free tip is to not over-edit your photos. It may be tempting to play around all the editing tools and filters, but keep it natural. Too much editing can ruin your images by removing the interesting details.

Digital Storage: Estimate that 100 pictures will take up about 200 MG, and 1000 photos will use about 2GB. (1000 B = 1KB, 1000KB = 1MB, 1000 MB = 1 GB, 1000Gb = 1 TB, 1000 TB = 1 Petabyte). Bring a lot of storage on your phone, or on a memory stick. You may need to remove old unwanted apps and videos ahead of time. Save this content elsewhere on a USB thumb drive or in the cloud. You don't want to get an error message which says your memory is used up in the middle of your shoot. Be prepared with twice the memory you expect to need. If you don't know your settings for storage, go to your carrier (ex. Verizon) or your device manufacturer (ex. Apple) and ask for help. The representative will tell you if you need more memory and how to clear your data and delete apps you are not using.

Tech and travel

Personal technology has changed travel forever. You can explore many ways to get familiar with technology on travel—before, during and after your trips. In addition to mobile devices, more data and tools are available. Beware of some applications which are collecting data about you. Apps on your phone collect location data if you enable the app to use your location. This can be all the time, or only when you're using the app. Some applications—like the map or compass—require your location for optimal performance. Some other apps don't need to always know where you are. Location tracking can be accurate because it knows where you go throughout the day and even where you live. However, you can turn off or manage this tracking from your phone privacy setting under Location Services.

Religion, spirituality and travel memories

Keeping your faith strong while on the road is important. You may be planning a mission trip as you read this book. If you're looking for religious community,, here are six tips for finding your spiritual guidance on the road:

1. Download the Church Finder app from the Apple store or Google Play, found in the USA App store.
2. Go to your search engine and type in "Churches near me." Or "Churches (location)." Check the ratings. Social media may have specific information you need, so you can also search.
3. Find Facebook groups in the city/village you visit and connect there. For example, search "Christians (location)." You will find several groups which may interest you.
4. Ask your spiritual friends before you go.
5. Ask your pastor for suggestions.
6. Find a trusted concierge in a hotel or restaurant you are visiting.

Before you attend a new religious or spiritual service, ask and learn about expectations, address, service times and dress codes. This guidance will help you create special travel memories from your faith and spiritual services.

How to save money along the way.

Saving money while you travel allows you to travel longer. Travel to where the locals go. It may be a bar, a café, the local library, or church. Find out what the local people do in their daily lives. You don't always need to visit the "touristy" places, just to claim you were there. Consider your personal needs, desires, and interests. Follow your own special interests and see where this takes you, away from the crowded tourist traps. Take a city bus or subway instead of a personal vehicle.

The best way to save money on travel expenses is to share a room with someone else. However, this doesn't always work well for solo travelers. Here are a few other tips to save your hard-earned cash:

- House swap
- Take a meal with you
- Travel via public transportation
- Have a feasible plan for your daily budget.
- Work as a traveling nurse or tutor on a cruise ship or dude ranch.
- Bring your work with you. If your job allows you to work remotely, take your "office" with you on the road to earn money.
- Eat a huge lunch. Later, you can have a snack for dinner which will likely satisfy you until morning
- Go grocery shopping instead of eating out

☐ Beware the "travelers" or "foreigner" tax when taking taxis or shopping at markets. Compare prices between stores, or use a metered app to estimate the total cost of your fare.

Step Two

Deciding which places to visit

For me, the weather should be ideal and agree with my comfort step for my trip to be enjoyable. The best seasons for solo travel should be considered, unless you choose other reasons. For those visits, you might prefer an off-season or 'shoulder' season, which means almost prime season, but not the best time to visit. Consider adding travel days on to a work-related trip. This allows you to leave earlier and return after business is concluded. Your travel expenses may be even lower for your employer, if you get a better deal on the airfare and hotel. For example, it may be less expensive to fly on a Tuesday instead of a Friday. It's always good to compare pricing before you purchase your ticket.

Do you plan visits to friends for the places you have an interest in seeing? They may be able to meet you and walk you around their favorite neighborhoods. Last year, when I was in Atlanta, I took a 3-day side trip to Nashville, Tennessee to see some honky-tonk music and the Grand Ole Opry. I called my friend Susan who lives outside of Nashville. She met me for lunch and showed me her downtown favorite spots including a semi-hidden alley with live country music. It wasn't mentioned in the city's travel guide. This is one method to learn about a city from a local's perspective while respecting their time and experience.

Visit a bookstore

On your travels, make time to visit a local bookstore. This has a certain charm and delight. Walk in and transport yourself to any section and start searching. You may find yourself in the "travel" section before long. Surround yourself with the culture of the store, and the history which lives in each of the books, just waiting to be read. What is the title of your favorite book on travel besides this one?

Arts and culture.

Start by reading a lot, and doing a little planning. Which arts most interest you? Is it music? If so, then you should consider seeing some live music on your trip. When I was in Hannibal, Missouri during the pandemic, the local town came to life on Monday nights with an orchestra playing on one side of the street and the audience listening on the other side. I was delighted with this unexpected classical concert experience with a nearly full orchestra playing requests. If you like sculpture, get informed about the best known or most interesting sculpture. If you prefer dance, research where the live dances are held. If you want to see a film, look out for big screen or small screen opportunities. Culture through music and art is a wonderful way to learn about a region, no matter the distance from home.

Reunions for independent travelers

Reunions don't sound "independent" to me. However, with a plan to be solo before and/or after you get together-it can be. If your family announces a "reunion," you can begin planning your solo activities before and/or after the event now, without permission from the group. The actual details don't need to be shared with others. You can just say, "Sorry, I'm busy." Plan ahead to see a nearby village, town, zoo, or museum, on your own. The space you create just for you will fill you with good memories and carry you a long way once your group's reunion begins. Our family reunions have been held in different locations, including a Christmas in Colorado skiing, a visit to the aquarium in Atlanta, lunch on the beach in California, and on a cruise to Mexico. For each of these family reunions, I had time for solo travel before, after or during the event. Be clear on what time you choose for yourself. Start planning your reunion adventure now, with the excitement for your solo trip within the reunion trip.

Step Three

Paper money and coins make good memories

Collect some coins and paper money on your journey. One of the things I will always remember about a country is the currency. Sometimes it's beautiful artwork. Other times it's just a special memory. Even if it's just a few dollars, you may want to give this as a gift to someone you love. It shows you thought of them and want to share some of the culture and economics of the country with them. As you pass on the currency, you will be able to tell a story or two to make your trip more tangible to an outsider.

Holiday travel

Celebrate the holidays of the local population. If you are in Canada and they have a holiday such as Canada Day (July 1), celebrate it. Wherever you are, adopt the culture and the manner of the celebration. Don't expect to celebrate the 4th of July outside of the USA.

Cutting tool for travel

Small and low-tech things you may find handy on the road include an Olfa Touch Knife. It's a small, compact retractable blade. You can find these in many DIY stores. It's used for cutting cords, opening boxes or envelopes, and hundreds of small projects. Once you have one, you'll want to travel with it all the time. My friend Sandra had one for 20 years. She says it's allowed on airplanes too. One Olfa Touch knife costs about $2.23—which is less than three dollars for a lifetime of easy snips.

Use an activity you love to select a destination

There may be a sport you love, like skiing. The activity took me to different resorts and mountain towns over a 50-year skiing career. I've skied at some of the best resorts in both North and South America, which made winter and summer travel delightful. Flight deals can become the trigger which makes you decide to travel independently. Review deals on the main travel websites like Skyscanner, Google Flights, Expedia, and Booking. You can still be an independent traveler and decide on a trip with friends. This is what my friends and I enjoyed for a 3-day houseboat trip to Lake Powell, near the Grand Canyon. You can make memories like this which will last for a lifetime.

What are my favorite women's sporting travel events?

Answer: My favorite sporting travel events are high school women's sports. I enjoy watching young women compete with strength they never knew they had. They stand out in competition with peers and against rivals from other locations. Some of my favorite travel days have been spent in the bleachers watching a softball game or water polo team compete.

Sports Travel

My favorite baseball stadiums include most of the big-league National and American League baseball parks. Growing up in New York, I went to Shea Stadium to see the Mets and Yankee Stadium, both in New York City. When I moved to Chicago, the Cubs and the White Sox became the home teams. Over the decades of travel, I have been to nearly every major league baseball stadium in the US. This is sports travel. Oftentimes, I went by myself, just for the fun of the game. These games create a dramatic rivalry between teams from two cities with fans who believe they help their team win. Seeing the major league playing field is a memorable experience. Watching the players compete through athletic endeavors is invigorating. The sounds, the smells, as well as the emotion and action are appealing to me as a traveling fan.

Women's sports are becoming more of a spectator event every year. Women's NBA teams and women's college basketball are showing up in the TV ratings with increasing frequency. Women's collegiate softball and soccer steal my attention every year. Sports are a uniting force for a solo traveler. The Olympics games are the ultimate travel sports events, especially for women's soccer and track and field events. Other sports with World Championships include Futbol, with the World Cup and qualifying events. I attended the summer 1984 Olympics in Los Angeles, CA. Being solo helped me buy someone's extra Olympics Track and Field Finals ticket at a discount. I hope you enjoy the Olympic experience in 2028, in Los Angeles, CA again. Consider going to the NFL trademarked Super Bowl, and the *World* Series (this comprises mostly teams from the US and Canada), the NCAA, WNBA and NBA Championships, the NHL as well as local high school, collegiate and club sports where you are traveling.

Step Four

Planning a Step Four trip may take extra effort. You might think about a visit to Mexico or a border crossing in El Paso, Texas. Some of the off-the-beaten-path destinations have been the most memorable. For example, most people will shop in Tijuana, just across the border from San Diego, in Mexico. If you drive just a bit further south, you will discover the beauty of Rosarito and see a whole new world of culture. The Rosarito Beach Hotel is in an area of town where you will feel safe, even willing to walk around alone.

Ancestry travel

Where are your ancestors from? This is a question all of us think about. Genealogy is the study of your family tree, showing the history of a family over several generations. Finding your family history can help you discover more about your own life. Traveling to places where you can unravel this discovery can be a challenge, but it is highly rewarding and exciting. Genealogy has gained popularity in recent years. Have you researched your ancestry? What would you be doing now if your ancestors never emigrated? I've been to Ireland, and I want to go back sometime and visit places where my relatives lived. You can start by looking at photographs of your parents and grandparents.

My grandparents came to the USA as immigrants on Ellis Island, New York, like so many others. Establish your family tree. Talk to all living relatives and ask simple questions about who your parents were, where they were born and stories about places they lived. You can check official records and research online to broaden your scope. Look for forums and genealogical societies. Independent travel works well for ancestry searches. Once you are in your country of origin, you can ask about distant relatives, visit the town hall and look up local records. You can speak to religious leaders, who may know about births and deaths. Doctors, notaries, and lawyers may also provide information. The local newspaper or library may offer help. You can also visit a marketplace and talk to the elderly who may be shopping there. The best free resources are Family Search from the Church of Latter-Day Saints (LDS). Based on your ancestry, you will find different resources. On a trip to Salt Lake City, we looked up our family history in the LDS library and found information going back two, three, and four generations. Set a time limit for yourself but have some fun learning. I have been to some of the places in Ireland where my grandparents talked about, but there's a lot more for me to see on my next visit to the Emerald Isle. Scotland has been on my bucket list for decades. Your origin can be a collective knowledge you and your relatives start reviewing on a regular basis.

Dreaming of a Step Four destination

If you were to take off for one year for travel, what continent would you visit? You could travel to Australia for less than a year, of course, but to get the full feel, you would also want to take a few months and visit nearby New Zealand.

You could start on the east coast in Sydney. Afterwards, you could travel north along the Gold Coast and see Surfers Paradise, then go to Brisbane, Cairns, visit Alice Springs and go to Ayers Rock. You could spend time in Perth, Melbourne, Tasmania, Adelaide—then go back to Sydney and see what you missed the first time. You may want to see Ayers Rock, or Uluru, close to the midpoint of the country where the closest city was Alice Springs. If you like the states of Colorado, Wyoming, and Utah, you'd like this area.

Step Five

How to choose a Step Five travel destination:

- ⬚ See where your reward points can take you.
- ⬚ Follow travel sites with advice and keep a running list.
- ⬚ Ask the most well-traveled people you know.
- ⬚ Pick an event to attend (not a destination).
- ⬚ Do something sporty. You could run a 10k race/swim at a beach.
- ⬚ See if you can book one-way tickets around the world.
- ⬚ Tap into Google Flights, Scotties or Skyscanner for flights.
- ⬚ Find out which family members want you to visit them in a foreign country.

My favorite place to travel so far

I have enjoyed all my travels, but if I had to pick just one, it would be Seychelles, which is an island nation far off the coast of East Africa, near Madagascar. I was there solo and all I had to research the town was a hand drawn map created by a friend, because this was before the internet. It is a worthwhile visit if you are independent and want to see a beautiful place which is not overrun with Americans.

VPN for Step Five travel

There are countries where you will need to download a Virtual Private Network (VPN) service before you can connect to Google or other apps. A VPN works by encrypting your data when you're using the internet. They are not all the same, with few standards and regulations. It can be hard to tell which ones are best. Top rated ones include ExpressVPN, NordVPN, and Surfshark.

Find places "off the beaten path"

Almost everyone loves the feeling of discovering a hidden paradise, being a part of something rare, new and refreshing—something away from the obvious. Here's how I find the non-typical sites: I read the guidebooks, research what other tours are doing, and then decide what matters. The first time I went to Paris, it was only for three days, and the Louvre Art Museum was closed on the day I would have gone. It was 20 years later when I returned to Paris. I still wanted to experience it, even though it's a popular tourist destination. After this visit to the art museum, I jumped on the subway in France, traveled to a distant part of the city and had a different experience. You may combine a touristy with a non-touristy activity each day for some variety.

The best ways to go off the beaten path are to ask the locals. When you are at a restaurant, café, or bar, ask the nearby guests to tell you their favorite hangouts, and tell them your interests. Many will respond to your genuine interest. Most of them would welcome a discussion with a newcomer. They want to share their favorite places. If you don't ask, you miss out on the opportunity. You'll only get what the "tour operator" wants you to experience. There's nothing wrong with a tour if it fits your agenda.

If you want to see Asia, you have the great cities of Beijing and Shanghai in China, as well as many other incredible cities like Tokyo and Kyoto in Japan. Tokyo, for example, is the world's biggest city. It has interesting fashion, food, museums and many unexpected treasures to explore. If you like Africa, consider traveling to Nairobi, Kenya, which is one of the most popular Safari destinations in Africa. There, you can explore the wildlife parks and reserves. You can also visit island nations such as Seychelles or Madagascar. Madagascar is known for its beautiful rainforests and breathtaking views of nature.

8 TRAVEL TIPS

Try a new kind of travel.

Maybe you're an urban traveler. Try a remote location for your next trip. If you usually visit National Parks, try a more indoor destination, such as a museum or river cruise for a change. Make your life more adventurous by going away from what's popular today and find yourself.

Kill insomnia with prayer

If you believe in prayers, are thinking about sleeping, but you're not in Slumberland yet, try to say your prayers. Once you start praying and concentrate on this, you'll often drift off to sleep and stay there.

Time management for travelers

Be in the moment and enjoy it. Don't try to be elsewhere. You will be more focused and have a better trip. You can work while on the road, and a little planning ahead can save a lot of troubles later. If you are working on projects while traveling, try to figure out the best time of day for you to be working, so you don't feel like you are working all day long. Depending on your work, you may be able to fit in both your travel and your projects.

Choosing between a beach or mountains

Which trip would you choose? If I had to select, it would be the beach. Hiking Torrey Pines State Park in Southern California is ideal because it's beside the beach and hilly too. Growing up in Long Island, New York, I always felt surrounded by water, even though the island is quite large and long. I really missed the ocean when I lived in the Midwest. The Midwest was relatively flat. In Southern California, there is plenty of ocean and mountains. I recommend you try this if you can do both: ski the mountains in the morning, and swim in the ocean/lake later in the day.

Memory tips

Remembering important names, dates and facts will help you travel better. As we get older, some of us lose our short-term memory, so how do we keep up with remembering names and important places during travel? Here is a list to help you to improve your memory while traveling:

- ☐ Say the names and places out loud. Look at the person whose name you wish to remember.

- ☐ Use as many senses as possible to indelibly store information in your memory.

- ☐ Try to remember something which rhymes with the word; for example, if it's "Nancy" think of "fancy."

☐ Remember phone numbers. This means seven digits plus at least three more. This is hard. Write it down in the Notes app on your phone. You can access it without Wi-Fi there.

Jam up a credit card thief

You may not know you've been compromised until it's too late. Be sure you have a plan in the event of losing your credit cards. There are some ways to get back at those who will try to steal your credit card info. First, keep track of your credit cards, the numbers and phone numbers of the banks. Protect your funds from theft by encasing credit cards in foil, using a special chipped card which jams up the would-be thief, or keep the cards in a Radio Frequency Identification (RFID) sleeve. Even if you're shopping in a store, a thief can steal your credit card info.

Journal in a notebook

Solo travelers should journal in a notebook. Each day on the road, say what you're grateful for. This collection will become a lasting memory. Your journal would hold more memories than the photographs taken. Words describe the feelings inside the heart—not just the two dimensions, but every dimension.

Souvenir tips

Souvenir is a word derived from French, which means "to remember or come to mind." It is an item or token kept in remembrance of an occasion, person or place. You acquire these for the memories which they bring—memories you can share or keep to yourself. The worst souvenirs are breakables, such as glass and fragile art, because they may not be practical to carry. Next to breakables are heavy things, such as books, bricks, or electronics. My favorite things to share with others are scarves, bookmarks, and photographs. My husband likes when I give him a rock from my trip. When I visited South Dakota, I gave him a small rock from the World-Famous Crazy Horse carved statue, which has been in development since the 1950s. He loved it. What are some of your favorite souvenirs? If it's practical, portable and necessary, there will be more motivation to collect it. Otherwise, it's junk.

Use social media safely

Don't tell people on social media you're gone if there's no one home. Your address is available to anyone. You want your home to look inhabited, so it will not stand out. It may be tempting to share your experiences on the go; however, it's in your best interest to not post photos of you on vacation far away as people can monitor your travel. It's best to wait until you're home. Then, you'll enjoy the adventure of your trip even more.

Casino safety

When in a casino, know where the exits are, find the best restaurants, and ask for any free services. Often you will get free rooms, free entertainment, and other benefits by membership in their loyalty programs. They all seem to have some special member benefits, so ask about these. Try to stay away from the smoking areas if you can as they are dirtier, and the air is not as good for you to breathe.

Lesson-Unsoaked sneakers

My sneakers got soaked while traveling. My feet were unhappy. If your shoes get wet and you need to dry them out, unlace them. They will dry faster. One tip I learned was to use a hair dryer. I should have bought a new pair of sneakers on the trip. This is a souvenir I would treasure with every step.

Have some travel fun

Things won't always go your way. The weather may not be what you expected. You may encounter a disaster, or you may fall sick. What can you do to make the most of it? This may be when you check in at home and tell someone you love about your troubles, so you feel better. Remember tomorrow may be better, and your attitude will improve.

Check the weather in advance

Check the weather report and have an alternative plan in mind. If you've booked an outdoor event and the weather is not cooperating, you need to have a backup plan. With today's Doppler Radar and other tools on your smartphone, (such as the Weather Channel), you can get microclimate weather by the hour and avoid surprises. Predicting the weather means you can already plan on a second choice in case your destination is unavailable. You should do your outdoor activities on sunny days. On days when the weather is gloomy, you can do your indoor activities, like shopping or seeing a museum.

Build memories one day at a time

When you travel, each day opens new possibilities. It's good to have a plan, but also remember plans change. Build your memories and plan your days with some flexibility and spontaneity.

Weather

When you plan your next trip, be sure to plan for weather emergencies. Check the weather forecast. Bring adequate clothing and footwear. You have a lot of choices for weather apps. These are listed in order of recommendations:

- Morecast.com gives you options by planning your route, adding locations, and timing your departure.

- Accuweather is rated #1 by popular science. It offers MinuteCast, a circular clock-like forecasting tool which alerts if it's going to rain in the next hour.

- Weather.gov

- Weather.com

- Driveweatherapp.com illustrates the National Weather Service's forecast, showing motorists weather, wind, temps and radar.

- Weatherbug.com

- Weatherroute.io

- Weather.gov/abr

- Weather underground

- Carrot Weather

- Google Play Weather

- Apple Store Road Trip

Double the Celsius temperature and add 15 points to convert to Fahrenheit.

Take national pride in your country

It's good to be confident in your native country. Remember that when you travel, you represent the country or region you are from. Be humble and ask about current cultural concerns, issues and pride moments. If you are from the USA, do not assume your country is the best or the worst. There have been times when I was embarrassed by the behavior of some from my country. Remember you are a guest, wherever you are from.

Store your luggage at a hotel

If you want to store your luggage for the day, go to a chain hotel where you are a member of the loyalty program and ask for the bell captain to store your luggage. They usually will do it for free, which means you can give them a healthy tip, so you don't need to carry it all day. This worked out so well for me last week in Chicago. I stored it at the Hilton Hotel downtown and was happy to retrieve it later on and tip the service person.

Summary:

Choose your destinations as a solo traveler and be where you see yourself thriving.

Journaling in your notebook and photography will enhance your travel experience.

Off the main or beaten path is preferred for solo travelers.

Traveling is fun, and be prepared for all flavors of fun.

Part B (soon to be released) of the book series offers you selected destinations you may want to visit. They are ranked based on the steps of the 5 Steps. The Step One section consists of regions of the USA, starting with the East Coast, Midwest and West Coast easy-to-reach travel destinations.

TRAVEL ADVICE SUMMARY

Tips for Coping with a Fear of Traveling

Although it is best to consult with a mental health professional for any phobia, many people find planning and organization can help combat mild symptoms of hodophobia.

Plan Your Route: If you are driving to your destination, sit down with a map and plan how far you will travel each day. Make hotel reservations and note the locations of nearby restaurants. If you are traveling by public carrier, such as a ship or a plane, confirm your bookings a few days before you leave. Allow plenty of time to arrive early and make a backup plan in case of delays.

Learn What to Expect in Advance: Search the Internet for information on your hotel. Look at deck plans for your cruise ship or seating charts for your plane or train. Learn where important facilities and amenities are located. Familiarize yourself with security procedures and be sure not to pack anything which is prohibited.

Visualize your Steps: In your mind's eye, picture yourself walking through all the major steps in your journey. Watch yourself stroll through the airport, sit at your gate, and board the plane. Imagine yourself effortlessly negotiating city traffic and finding the perfect parking spot. Visualizing success builds confidence and reduces stress.

Rest, Relax and Hydrate: Get plenty of sleep in the days leading up to your trip. Carry water throughout your journey along with a few salty snacks. Exhaustion and dehydration make it more difficult to confront challenges.

9 Lessons Learned

Food Poisoning

I ate Udon noodles with shrimp in the 1221 Restaurant near the Taroko Gorge in Taiwan and was awfully sick for a full night—the full bucket experience you don't want to ever have. Don't eat shellfish if you have any doubts about the food. This was a fancy restaurant, but we were in a hurry, so they did not cook the food all the way through. Don't ask to have your food in a hurry if it is shellfish.

The wrong hole in one.

I was traveling and enjoying a visit at a golf course that was not busy at all. I hit my golf ball on the 12th tee. I lost the ball, so I had to take a penalty and start with a second ball. Then on the 15th hole, my original ball was found in the cup. No one had been playing between these holes. It had landed there about 20 minutes earlier. So strange, but still a lesson learned that I found my lost ball, but did not get a hole in one. Still the trip was fun because I can tell the story of a surprise find of a ball in the cup. The lesson is that you may find your lost items where you least expect them.

Getting a boat tow can be welcome

Here's the situation—I was in a canoe rowing the same stretch of water for what seems like hours. The current was too strong, and it was impossible to keep going in the same direction. This was on Long Island, and it was a 3-day canoe trip. Getting a tow from a nearby speedboat not only helped us move forward, it also gave us confidence we needed to finish our trip. In the long run, the lesson was about asking for help, getting the help we needed and then moving forward to complete the journey.

Broken fingernails

These may not seem like a big deal to some people, but breaking a nail can be a real challenge. I've suffered this many times, so here's my lesson for you. I've had bruises, bleeding, and infection. You don't want this. If you have acrylic or fake nails, you should try to go to a salon and get it repaired, of course. I had a broken fingernail and had to cut it down so it would not be infected later. The lesson was to clip my nails short before I left for my trip. I had to do the regular maintenance to keep them looking good. Keep fingernails short if you plan to travel.

Ask for help when you need it

Sometimes when I travel, I don't ask for help, but I should. One of the things which keeps me stuck is my smartphone. Sometimes, I don't have my settings right; for example, the app may be turned off, so I can't get it working. I may be too determined to do it myself, so I don't ask for help.

Don't be like me. Ask for help if you get stuck. It may be that you just need to go to YouTube and search for "How to XYZ" to figure it out yourself.

Don't give up too easily

It took me nearly 40 tries to learn how to windsurf in Fiji. It was on the 40th try when I finally learned how to make the sail sing! Don't get discouraged because it may take you a long time. Once you get it and learn the basics, you'll be sailing or doing what you are determined to complete.

Double-check your room key number

I came back from the pool and went to the wrong hotel. I haven't learned from my mistakes yet. The key did not work. I had some earlier problems with the key, so I assumed the same problem happened. It was my error. I called the front desk to help with the key, then looked at the room number, and saw I was one building away from mine. So, I tried to call back, but was put on hold. I went to my building and called again. Before anyone answered, a person came off the elevator to help me. I was so embarrassed and guilty. I thought the key was wrong, but it was just me in the wrong building.

Don't trust the balloon pilot

I went on safari alone. Well, I did meet friends on the plane. One was a girlfriend who I still consider a good pal, even though we have not seen each other lately. The other was a balloon pilot—let's call him Bob. Bob invited me to his camp to ride a hot air balloon. About a week after arriving in Nairobi, I landed in his camp and he was delighted, but said I had to sleep with him to get the balloon ride. I declined, found a proper tent and slept there alone. I never saw him again, until watching the Today show on NBC. Morning host Bryant Gumbel was on a balloon ride with Bob. It was the same guy. I wonder if he had to sleep with him. The lesson learned was my lack of judgment because I had trusted him.. I believed in Bob, until I was confronted with his alternate romantic agenda, but the lesson was learned. Don't over trust an expert who offers assistance.

When skiing, avoid the last run of the day

Never take the 'last run' of the day skiing. Save some energy for tomorrow, or the road down the mountain. Always tell yourself you have one more run, so you will not try to push yourself past your abilities. We often hurt ourselves on the last run, so quit before you are finished and injured. I was at Copper Mountain, and my friends were all better skiers, so I took the easier way down, and was in a hurry to catch up. I took a bad fall and ended up snapping my knee, and later learned it was my ACL. It was painful, and I was unable to ski all the way down, so the ski patrol had to take me down the hill.

Avoid seedy parts of town

I almost never get accosted when I'm traveling. Most people have been especially nice and thoughtful to me. However, here's what happened to my friend, a seasoned traveler. She was walking in a large downtown city, a construction zone, so the sidewalk was narrow. It was at nighttime, and someone walked up to her, asked her a question, and then took her entire backpack and ran away with it. Don't let this happen to you.

Wear bike shorts

If you like to ride a bicycle, and decide you want to take a long ride, be sure you wear your special bike shorts with the extra padding that cushions the lower body. I had a 25-mile ride and did not wear the bike shorts. I was sorry about this for days afterwards and all I needed was to change into my padded shorts in advance. Be smart and wear the proper clothing with padded bike shorts.

Don't speak badly to the TSA

I said some improper words while I was in the security line at an airport in Colorado. I was by myself in high school at the time. No one got hurt, but this showed my immaturity. Be careful what you do when going through any security situation. I'm embarrassed about this, and I was warned and never did it again.

Check that you leave the restaurant with your own credit card

I was in a restaurant in Hawaii with a family group. We enjoyed a buffet dinner, and the same bill, so we handed in our credit cards and the waitress split the check. After adding a tip and signing, we left. My credit card would not work when I wanted to buy gas later on, but I didn't overthink it. I went sightseeing at the zoo, and more. While paying for dinner the following night, I noticed my credit card was my brother-in-law's, who had the same last name and credit card company, so they looked alike. Once we figured it out, this took a while to settle, mail the cards back and pay the difference in what I had spent. The lesson is to check your credit card name to make sure you got yours back from the server.

Choose the greater adventure

I should have gone scuba diving in the Great Barrier Reef, off the coast of Australia. If you are certified as a scuba diver, then take advantage of this credential. My friend was not certified, so we both went snorkeling on the trip. However, I have since wished I had tried the scuba instead. Once you're certified, you are certified for life, and you can take refresher courses to practice if you don't remember the basics. I had the opportunity, but I did not take it. Do what you can to scuba dive if the opportunity presents itself.

Daylight pickpockets

My friend Becky wanted me to share her story. She told me about getting robbed right after she got to Europe, because she was a little jet lagged and not herself. Her friend had her wallet in a purse, zipped, and inside the jacket—closed. They were on the subway, and it was crowded, but she didn't even know they were picked. This is a sign of a good pickpocket because she never saw it happen. Prevent robberies with zipped pockets on the inside of jackets, and backpacks that are not easily cut. Sling your satchel across your body instead of a shoulder strap. Don't get robbed. Be conscious of your surroundings. The end of the story was they got their wallets back, but all the cash was gone. They did have to cancel their credit cards, and the bank was helpful, giving them some personal support and advice for the future.

Poison ivy

Poison ivy is a lesson learned and I've finally learned my lesson. I got it bad. I was hiking in a National Forest in the middle of a sunny day in the summer. Little did I know I had the oils on my hands and was spreading it all over my body in the humidity.

Ask in advance if you don't know

One day in Hong Kong, I wanted to see live horse racing. I asked about where it was held and then took public trains and buses to get there. I paid admission and went to the viewing areas and planned to watch the horses, however, it was off track betting. The horses were only on TV here, even though there were thousands of other people there enjoying racing and gambling. I wish I had known this in advance. I did not ask the right questions, so I was disappointed. Ask the questions in advance.

Regulate your body temperature

As I write this, I'm overheating. I'm in need of a cool down. There's no reason to overheat. Here are some cool down tricks. Find a towel and put water on it. Drape it around your neck and face. You will instantly feel relief.

Plan for travel finances properly

Paying high credit card foreign transaction fees was a financial error. When buying with a credit card, always ask for the transaction to be made in the local currency, to avoid some fees.

Forgetting the essentials

Not doing my packing homework has left me without a bathing suit. I love to swim, so that's an essential in my suitcase or backpack. If you like to swim, pack your suit.

Respect laws about currency in other countries

Certain people in Kenya airport did not want to give up their money to the Kenyan police. This did not happen to me, but I want to warn others about how people feel about money in other countries, such as Kenya. There was an American youth—let's call him Robert—who was found trying to leave the country with Kenyan dollars. Normally, the Kenyan's airport official's job is to protect their currency, so Kenya keeps any cash found on outgoing airline passengers. This passenger did not want to give up his cash, and tried to burn it, but was caught and sent to prison in Kenya. Several days after being imprisoned, he appealed to the US consulate to be freed. It was a terrible experience for Robert. So, please, convert your cash into your currency before you leave Kenya. They did take about $10 US from me, in Kenyan cash, and I let them keep it. They found my cash easily. I was using it as a page marker/bookmark in the paperback novel I was currently reading. I wasn't hiding it. Your experience may be different.

Visit Minnesota when it's not frozen

I visited Minneapolis in January. Visit Minneapolis when you consider the weather appropriate. In January, the daily high temperature is 24 Fahrenheit (-5 Centigrade) and low is 10 degrees Fahrenheit (15 Centigrade). I have been back to Minnesota many times in spring, summer and fall and loved it there. If you live in a cold climate, you may travel to warmer places in winter.

Getting new brakes when all I needed was a battery

This was an expensive lesson and recently, it still hurts. I started my car and was ready for a trip, then my car told me it would not go, loud and clear. The one error message was no brakes. So, I called the dealership and told them the problem and had it towed there for inspection. The car had about 60k mileage and was still under a 100k warranty. They insisted it needed a whole new brake system, and the cost would be $3k. I shopped around on several car dealer websites and was unable to find any information on my issue. I negotiated a deal for fifteen hundred dollars, and agreed. They installed new brakes. A few months later, the same thing happened again, and the dealership asked me to tow it in. Instead, I called a tow truck and they sold me the new battery and installed it. This lesson was auto franchise dealerships want to sell you things you don't need. It was the battery all along. The dealership was wrong, but I'm not able to prove anything. I should have had another professional opinion.

Take the trip you'd regret NOT going on

I regret not going on Spring Break, the ski trip to the Alps, and the Wedding in Italy. These and 100 others are trips I did not get to take. If you have a trip you want to take, and have the time and the money, don't wait until it's too late. Enjoy while you can.

Stop for the STOP sign

I did not stop, but I was slow. I was ticketed, and officially, still in the middle of the intersection. This indicates how slow the car was moving. I was looking for a parking spot, exactly where the motorcycle officer was parked on my left, hiding behind a parked car. There were no other drivers on the road, so I got the ticket in Del Mar, California. It was more than $300, and I paid it and went to driver's education training so I could get the infraction removed from my record. If you get a ticket, I recommend this as well.

Parking tickets

I clearly remember paid parking across the street was about $40 for the night and it seemed high, so I chose to keep looking for a parking spot. In the long run, I should have just paid for it. Instead, I paid twice and then had to wait several months for a refund on one of them. The "NO PARKING" sign was faded and worn out. It was hard to read what was written on it—if it was 8p.m. or 6pm. Most of the downtown parking spots in the area have this problem. 8 and 6 look a lot alike at night. Don't be like me. Look carefully at the signage, or take a picture of it while inspecting it.

Losing my parked car

I have lost my car more than once, while it was parked. This can happen anywhere, but especially in a parking garage. One time, I was parked at a shopping mall in downtown San Diego and I could not find my car. The parking lot was confusing. I searched for my car for what seemed like an hour. They have even and odd floors, but I did not know it when I parked. Now, I'm careful to walk back to my car the same way I left it. I don't try to take shortcuts. When you park your car, don't be like me and lose it.

Unmatched shoes

The wrong shoe. I packed my suitcase in the dark and brought one navy shoe and one black shoe. They looked similar in the dark but in the daylight, they were clearly different. Don't pack in the dark like I did. Bring pairs of shoes when you travel.

Don't break your axle

I was driving the company car in Chicago as I was visiting a client. After my appointment, I got in the car, but was unable to drive as the axle was broken. No one had done any maintenance on the car and the axle just split. The car would not go, so I had to call a cab and come back to the office to explain the car couldn't move and needed a tow.

Losing jewelry on the road

Walking through a small town in Alaska, I felt a chain from my necklace in my sleeve. This was not a good sign. It indicated my special cross from my necklace had broken and was missing. I have the chain, but not the pendant. The lesson learned was to buy a better chain with a new clasp. I had prior warnings, and I should have done something. Replace your old clasp before you lose the pendant.

Hiking alone

This happened to my friend, Jan, and she asked me to include it in this book. She went on a solo hike and had a terrible accident. She blacked out with a concussion, broken nose—and her knee and mouth were all torn up. Her face was lacerated, and she wants to share this advice: Don't hike alone. Jan, we all wish you fast healing and thank you for the lesson.

Carry your luggage in one trip

Don't bring too much. If you can't carry it all in one trip, you have too much stuff. Only bring what you need and leave the rest behind. I've taken too much stuff on my trips before, and wished I had left half behind.

Forgetting my suitcase on a car trip

On a three-day car trip with my 1-year-old daughter and husband, we remembered the diaper bag, but forgot the suitcase to bring to the car. We had enough diapers and made sure we washed our own clothes daily, then put them back on. We were barely able to manage these three days. When we returned home, the suitcase was right where we left it, inside the front room. Don't forget your suitcase.

Forgetting something important in transit

I drove to the airport with my 16-year-old son, for a weeklong trip to Colorado. When we arrived at the airport, his suitcase was not in the car. It was packed, but back at the house. Luckily, we had enough time to drive there, get it, drive back and still make the flight. Don't forget your suitcase or important documents for a flight like this.

Hot Spicy Foods while traveling

When I travel, I've learned about eating hot spicy foods the hard way. I've tried to swallow some hot sauce, pizza with hot peppers, and chile relleno which were hot and spicy. I prefer no spice. It may sound boring, but I learned my lesson the hard way. Now, I just say "no", which is empowering. In the US, people are using much more spice than they used to. This is changing due to immigration from Asia and Latin America. For others, spices can be a way to broaden your global horizons.

If you liked these lessons and want more. you can send me your email and I will update you to receive more details on the next books in the series, including Part B, 5 Steps to Solo Travel.

info@drmarytravelbest.com

10 BONUS Lessons Learned

Getting a tow can be okay

Here's the situation, I was in a canoe rowing the same stretch of water for what seems like hours. The current was too strong, and it was impossible to keep going in the same direction. This was a Girl Scout camp on Long Island, and it was a 3-day canoe trip. Getting a tow from a nearby speedboat not only helped us move forward, it also gave us confidence we needed to finish our trip. In the long run, the lesson was healthy.

Revenge of Montezuma

I drank a can of juice from a vending machine at the US-Mexico border. I was sick for three days. Be careful what you eat and drink, even if you drink it in the USA.

Last run of the day skiing

Never take the last run of the day skiing. Always say you have one more run, so you will not try to use every ounce of energy. We always hurt ourselves on the last run, so don't have one. I was at Copper Mountain, and my friends were all better skiers, so I took the easier way down, and was in a hurry to catch up. I took a bad fall and ended up snapping my knee. It was painful, and I was unable to ski all the way down, so the ski patrol had to take me down the hill.

Slow down on the bike going downhill

One of my big lessons learned was going downhill on a bike too fast. Even though I was on my brakes, I was going too fast for conditions. I was in Torrey Pines State Park, and the huge Torrey Pines tree had a big shadow over a tree root. And there were a lot of people walking uphill as I was going down. I flipped, and don't remember much more until I was sitting up and unable to walk. Yes, I broke my hip. The helmet saved my life. So, don't ride without one.

Lack of travel planning

Not enough time for my travel connection in the airport has made me miss a flight. Not doing my packing homework has left me without a bathing suit, Not preparing for my arrival has made my wait longer leaving the airport, not checking immigration requirements could have had serious consequences, and paying high credit card foreign transaction fees was a financial error. When buying with a credit card, always ask for the transaction to be made in the local currency, to avoid some fees.

Heal my dry skin

I suffer from dry skin; it's seasonal. Some have it year-round. I use creams and lip balm to keep my skin moist and reduce my chances of infection. If you have had any kind of rash or skin irritation, you may have an allergy. If your skin seems to be dry a lot, be sure to do what I do, keep drinking a lot of water and apply a sealant like Aquaphor or Be Well branded body balm to your dry skin to make them feel supple and soft.

Faith over Fear

Fear. I was afraid. It's the opposite of faith. I was afraid when I was lost and alone in Shanghai, China. I've made many lessons learned in travel, but I am thankful for them, because I've learned to make them about joy instead. I have not lived in the present for a long time. This is a part of travel which I need to work on. Live for now and maybe concentrate on being with those you are with more instead of looking at the future so much.

Getting Soaking Wet

Today I took a hike in the pouring rain. Yes, I got wet, of course. But it wasn't so bad because I expected to get wet. The forecast was for rain, so I had time to be prepared. If you're going to get out there in nature, you're surely needing to adjust for the elements. The lesson I learned was to have an umbrella nearby or handy, wear the right footwear, and take off the wet clothes quickly.

Getting seasick while fishing sharks

Sharks bite late at night, I'm told. I went on a fishing trip at 6pm in the Pacific Ocean. I got nauseous and should have taken a seasick pill before I went on the boat. Once you're on the boat, it's too late. Maybe my sickness helped attract some sharks. I did end up catching a 4-foot blue shark, and by the time I got off the boat, I was feeling much better. Don't get seasick like me. Take your meds a half hour before you board the vessel.

Losing my sunglasses on the water while boating.

How did I lose them? I've lost several pairs of glasses, and it's from being careless out on the water. My glasses sunk to the bottom and there was no way for me to get them back. Don't forget the floating sunglass flotation devices. You can add buoys to your croakies (i.e., the strings which help glasses stay on), depending on the weight and size of your glasses.

Leave ten minutes early for meeting a friend

I want to leave ten extra minutes as a buffer just in case I'm late. My friends used to say, "She'll be late for her wedding." Well, I have been better since then. But this is a lesson which I'll be learning throughout my lifetime.

My "short cut" through South Dakota

The best drive from Fargo, North Dakota to Sturgis, South Dakota could have been interstate, but I chose to take a scenic left turn in Bismarck and head south. A few hours later, I saw a small sign which said "locals only" but it was temporary, so I thought I'd try it. 25 miles in, I was forced to turn around because the Sioux Indian tribe set up a checkpoint to keep outsiders away. I had to drive 50 extra miles, which added extra time to a long drive. I ended up arriving at my destination, just a little bit later than I had planned. Don't try to drive through an Indian reservation during the COVID-19 pandemic. Go around. You'll be arriving at a more reasonable time.

Refundable travel losing money from Covid travel.

Many of us have lost money from bookings which could not be used due to COVID-19. The lesson learned from this is to buy refundable tickets for any reason, and always read and document the fine print. You have support for your claim, if the vendor doesn't want to refund your ticket, for whatever you purchased in advance.

Wearing a mask upside down

When I first put on my mask, I had it on upside down. I walked out of the house wearing the mask incorrectly, and the first person who saw me told me so. So now I learned my lesson, the metal strip goes over your nose, and it should be comfortable.

Follow Directions

The fastest way down the hill may not be a straight line. When you're solo, you need to rely on others and directions. So, try not to head out too far on your own if you don't know the terrain. A friend's brother went out for a hike straight down a big hill, which sounded like a good idea to him. It was in Palm Springs at the top of the scenic tram, which only takes minutes to go up. The clearly marked road down was recommended, but he tried to go straight down, over the brush and got stuck. Days later, we had to send helicopters out looking for him. He was found alive. Lesson learned. Follow directions.

Concluding remarks:

Be sustainable in your thoughts, in your actions, and in your intent.

Start small. Little things make a difference as they add up on your travels.

Slow travel is good travel.

"There is no shame in prioritizing and slowing down vs. overdoing. Most injuries happen when people are rushing. "Go slower, arrive sooner" is a helpful mantra." (Ellen McCabe, sister)

"Once in a while it really hits people that they don't have to experience the world in the way they have been told to." Alan Keightley

`Tourists are vulgar, vulgar, vulgar' (Henry James, quoted Pearce and Moscardo 1986:21)

A traveler is a stranger/ One of the delusions of the tourist, usually buffered from reality, is that he or she is a friend and even perhaps a benefactor of the locals. (Paul Theroux, Tao of Travel) p. 120

Otherness can be like an illness; being a stranger can be analogous to experiencing a form of madness.

Sightseeing is the art of disappointment (Stevenson- The Silverado Squatters)

A voyage is a piece of autobiography at best (The Cevennes Journal, 1978)

Little do you know your own blessedness: for to travel hopefully is a better thing than to arrive, and the true success is to labor" Virginibus Puerisque. P 12

Special thanks to: Ellen McCabe, Tina Shubat, Catherine Shubat, Sara Jones (RIP, 2021), Others to thank include Ben J. Shapiro and Wade Taylor for coaching and suggestions of Dr Mary Travelbest podcast.

Book readers and editors: Liz Myers (my high school English teacher), Kathy Tiernan, Andrea Glass, Pam Charboneau, Vikki Walton, Raquel Giraldez, Karla Scott, Leslie Joseph, Nancy Castaldo, Angali Bhardwaj, and Alice Daly, plus countless others. Global Editors from 6 countries included: Johanna Higgs, Cynthia Nhadi, Jennylin Garcia, Abigail Gordon, Atifa, Annie Percik and Rebecca Crowe.

REFERENCES:

deBecker, Gavin (1997) *The Gift of Fear: Survival Skills that Protect us from Violence*. Dell Publishing.

Theroux, Paul (2011) The TAO of TRAVEL

Note: This is not written by a medical doctor. Any advice should be considered along with other expert opinions.

Bonus: Additional COVID Travel

Vaccine Passports

You may need a vaccine related health passport in the future. Remember, rules change often, so be flexible with your schedule if possible and be patient as the world opens to more travel in the future.

History of Face Masks

Health-related facial coverings and masks have been around for more than 400 years, serving Plague Doctors in the 1700s and more recently to thwart other bacteria, and even air pollution. They have become a fashion statement and even how you wear yours says a lot about you as a person. Women used to wear veils which protected against dust, often with bacteria, in the 19th century. In the early 20th century, a widespread flu epidemic brought this facial covering to hospitals and the public once again. In March 2020, it was not common to see people wearing facemasks in the USA, but it has been common in many Asian countries for decades. I was in Shanghai, China in 1988, and I saw a lot of people wearing masks to protect others. This has become more common in many countries with COVID as well as air quality concerns. Perhaps, we have learned some lessons from Asian colleagues about wearing masks for many reasons, to protect others as well as themselves. The most effective face coverings are the N95 surgical masks, and the least effective are the cloth bandanas, but at least this is something to protect you. Due to COVID, you may not feel safe in someone's Airbnb. You may prefer a hotel with a full-time cleaning staff. Read the reviews before you book. If you're staying only one night, it may not be worth your stay, but if you're staying several days or a week, this can be a good way to travel independently and still feel home away from home.

ABOUT THE AUTHOR

Dr. Travelbest wrote the **World's First Guide to Independent Travel** and self-published it as a world travel tool in 1993. Since this publication, possibly up to a billion miles have been recorded by people who have read, listened to book recordings/podcasts, and followed on social media—people who are going places on planes, trains, autos, bikes, boats, and on foot, and one day in space exploration.

Dr. Mary Beth McCabe wanted to center her focus on the travel mission of bringing the world closer to peaceful living, rather than personal identity. Hence, she published under the pseudonym "Dr. Travelbest" in 1993. The mission will be continued by her daughter and avid global traveler and contributor, Ms. Christina Shubat—and by future generations of travelers like you.

Dr. McCabe has a Doctorate degree from a globally focused university and for three decades has owned a marketing/media agency, serving Fortune 500 companies with cross-cultural marketing and digital strategies. She is a world-renowned leader in marketing and has been a professor at ten universities throughout her career. McCabe is currently a Professor of Marketing at Point Loma Nazarene University. She has traveled to all 50 US states and more than 25 countries. She has traveled solo or with a friend to every continent except Antarctica. She is co-author of Mobile Marketing Essentials (Stukent, Inc), the first textbook on this topic. She lives in San Diego with her husband, Allen.

Made in the USA
Thornton, CO
05/08/22 13:50:54